S0-AIC-304

LOVE, HATE AND EVERYTHING IN BETWEEN

LOVE, HATE AND EVERYTHING IN BETWEEN

EXPRESSING EMOTIONS IN JAPANESE

Mamiko Murakami

Translated by
Ernest Reiss

KODANSHA INTERNATIONAL
Tokyo • New York • London

Distributed in the United States by Kodansha America, Inc., 114 Fifth Avenue, New York, N.Y. 10011, and in the United Kingdom and continental Europe by Kodansha Europe Ltd., 95 Aldwych, London WC2B 4JF. Published by Kodansha International Ltd., 17-14 Otowa 1-chome, Bunkyo-ku, Tokyo 112, and Kodansha America, Inc.

Copyright © 1997 by Kodansha International Ltd.
All rights reserved. Printed in Japan
First edition, 1997
97 98 99 00 9 8 7 6 5 4 3 2 1
ISBN 4-7700-2089-9

CONTENTS

PREFACE

Through teaching Japanese to non-native speakers, as well as editing a number of dictionaries and what have you, I've become somewhat particular about words. Japanese is as rich as any language in its ability to express the spectrum of human emotion. There are any number of ways, for example, to describe love for someone or something—depending upon whom or what is loved, how powerful that love is, and so on. This book is principally concerned with words and expressions that pertain to love and hatred.

I wonder what percentage of Japanese husbands, when told what a lovely wife they have, would respond, "Thank you. I think so, too." And how many would reply "Of course I do" to the question, "You love your wife very much, don't you?" For the most part, they'd be more likely to belittle their wives with answers like, "Are you kidding? You wouldn't want to see her without makeup! She can't cook, either," or "No, I made a big mistake when I married her."

A bigger mistake, of course, would be to accept such statements at face value, when they're actually just a facade to mask real feelings of affection. The diffidence that is such a part of social interaction in Japan has resulted in deprecation being elevated almost to an art form.

At first I wondered if, since Japanese so dislike being disliked, expressions of "hatred" weren't relatively few. In the course of compiling material for this book, however, I soon realized that that wasn't the case at all. I was confronted with a truly astonishing volume of common expressions for everything from mild distaste to absolute abhorrence. This though all anyone really wants is to be loved …

Tolstoy's observation, in *Anna Karenina*, that "All happy

families are alike; each unhappy family is unhappy in its own way" may also be true, at least in Japan, for expressions of love and hate. Perhaps, to paraphrase the great writer, it's simply a case of all pleasant feelings being alike and each unpleasant feeling being unpleasant in its own way.

In any event, the reader will find herein an abundance of ways to express every nuance of love, hatred, and everything in between. Emphasis has been placed on selecting the most commonly heard expressions and illustrating them with simple and natural-sounding sample sentences, to facilitate their immediate use in everyday conversation. It is my greatest hope that you will find this book invaluable when it comes to whispering words of love or declaring war.

In closing I would like to offer special thanks to Yumiko Kawamoto, who provided invaluable advice throughout the course of this project.

Mamiko Murakami
February 1997

はじめに

日本語を外国人に教えたり、また、辞書などの編集をしてきた経験上、多少なりともことばに対してのこだわりを持ってきました。

言語にはそれぞれ豊かな表現があり、日本語も他の言語に劣らず、豊かな感情表現を持っています。同じ「愛する」でも、対象はだれなのか、どの程度愛しているかなどによって、さまざまな言い回しが使われます。

この本では、原則として、人に対する愛情と憎しみに基づいていることば・表現にしぼって取り上げました。

「君の奥さんはすてきな人だね」と言われて、「ありがとう、そうなんだよ」という夫が日本人の何割いるでしょう。また「奥さんのことをとても愛してるんでしょう？」と聞かれて「もちろんですよ」とまじめに答える夫も多くはないはずです。大概は「冗談じゃないよ、化粧を落としたら見られたもんじゃないよ、それに飯もまずいし」とか「いやあ、まちがって結婚しちゃったんだよ」などと、けなすにちがいありません。

もちろんこれは表面上のことばであって、まともに受け取ってはいけません。謙遜や照れの気持ちが、愛情表現を内に隠して作り上げた「けなし上手」なのですから。

当初は、日本人は人に悪く思われたくなくて、「憎しみ」の表現はあまり多くないのではと考えていました。しかし、データを集めるうちに驚くほどさまざまな「憎しみ」をぶつけていることが分かってきました。本当は、みんな愛を求めているはずなのに……。

かの文豪の「幸福な家庭はみな一様に似通っているが、不幸な家庭はいずれもとりどりに不幸である」との言は、愛と憎しみの表現に関しては（少なくとも日本では）あたっているのかもしれません。

いずれにせよ、愛情表現も憎しみの表現も、日常会話にすぐ使えるよう平易で自然な用例にしてありますので、ことば豊かに大いに愛を語り、また、ののしりあうのに役立てていただけるものと思います。

最後になりましたが、本書を執筆するにあたって貴重なアドバイスをくださって河元由美子さんに心より御礼を述べたいと思います。

1997年2月　村上真美子

PART 1

FROM UNCERTAINTY
TO LOVE

AMBIVALENCE

Mā-mā まあまあ So-so; not particularly good, but not bad, either.

➡ 「彼のこと好きなの？」
「まあまあってとこかな」

"Kare no koto suki na no?"
"Mā-mā tte toko ka na."

"Do you like him?"
"He's all right, I guess."

➡ 母： （写真を見ながら）「どう、この人、なかなかいいじゃない？」
息子： 「まあまあだね」
父： 「いいかげんにしろ！ 選り好みしている年じゃないだろう！ これが最後の見合いのチャンスだぞ！」

Haha: (shashin o minagara) Dō, kono hito, nakanaka ii ja nai?
Musuko: Mā-mā da ne.
Chichi: Ii kagen ni shiro! Erigonomi shite iru toshi ja nai darō! Kore ga saigo no miai no chansu da zo!

Mother: (looking at a photograph) How about it? She looks pretty good, don't you think?
Son: Just so-so, I'd say.
Father: That's quite enough out of you! At your age, you're in no position to be choosy! This is your last chance to find a wife!

Manzara de mo nai まんざらでもない To be not completely averse to; to be clearly pleased at having one's ego stroked

➡ A: 「彼にあなたの気持ちを伝えたら、まんざらでもなさそうだったわよ」
B: 「えっ！ 本当？」
A: 「あとは、押しの一手よ」

A: Kare ni anata no kimochi o tsutaetara, manzara de mo nasa sō datta wa yo.

B: E! Honto?

A: Ato wa, oshi no itte yo.

Girl A: He certainly didn't seem displeased when I told
him about how you felt.

Girl B: Really?

Girl A: So go for it!

➺ 次期社長はあなたをおいてほかにないといわれて、専務は
まんざらでもない様子だった。

*Jiki shachō wa anata o oite hoka ni nai to iwarete, senmu
wa manzara de mo nai yōsu datta.*

When the managing director was told that he was the only
one who could possibly be appointed the company's next
president, he looked pretty pleased with himself.

Nikukarazu omou 憎からず思う (Lit., "not think someone detestable") To be not without feelings for. (⚹ Often
implies a deep fondness.)

➺ シェリルも彼のことを憎からず思っていたので、交際を申
し込まれたときは、すぐにOKした。

*Sheriru mo kare no koto o nikukarazu omotte ita no de,
kōsai o mōshikomareta toki wa, sugu ni OK shita.*

Cheryl kind of liked him too, so she agreed right away
when he asked if they could start seeing each other.

➺ 憎からず思っていた彼女からの電話に、サムはどきどきした。

*Nikukarazu omotte ita kanojo kara no denwa ni, Samu wa
dokidoki shita.*

Sam's heart started racing when he got a call from the girl
who'd been so much on his mind lately.

Myaku ga aru 脈がある (Lit., "there is a pulse") There's
a chance that things will work out; there is some hope; the
situation should not be written off yet.

➺ 彼女がプレゼントをすんなり受け取ってくれたってことは、
脈があるかも……

*Kanojo ga purezento o sunnari uketotte kureta tte koto wa,
myaku ga aru ka mo …*

She was so happy to get that present from you, you just might have a chance …

➠ A: 「彼女、仕事がすごく忙しいらしくって、なかなかデートのOKがでないんだ」

B: 「それって多分、脈ないね」

A: Kanojo, shigoto ga sugoku isogashii rashikutte, naka-naka dēto no OK ga denai n' da.

B: Sore tte tabun, myaku nai ne.

Guy A: She's so busy with her work, I can't get her to agree to a date with me.

Guy B: In that case, I'd say your chances are kind of slim.

FLATTERY

Homeru ほめる To praise, to compliment; to speak highly of.

➠ 私は、友達に親切だと先生にほめられた。

Watashi wa, tomodachi ni shinsetsu da to sensei ni home-rareta.

The teacher said I was kind to my friends.

➠ 彼は、いつも私の髪がきれいだとほめてくれる。

Kare wa, itsumo watashi no kami ga kirei da to homete kureru.

He's always telling me how pretty my hair is.

➠ A: 「君って、優しくて、親切で、友達思いで……」

B: 「おだてて、何をさせようっていうの？」

A: 「ええっ？　ほめているんだよ……」

A: Kimi tte, yasashikute, shinsetsu de, tomodachi-omoi de …

B: Odatete, nani o saseyō tte iu no?

A: Ē? Homete iru n' da yo …

Friend A: You're so gentle, kind and thoughtful …

Friend B: What's with the flattery? You must want something from me.

Friend A: Me? No! Just giving you a compliment.

RESPONDING TO COMPLIMENTS

あなたのお兄さん、とってもすてきね。
ありがとう。でも、残念ながら売約済みだよ。

"Anata no oniisan, tottemo suteki ne."
"Arigatō. De mo, zannen nagara baiyaku-zumi da yo."

"Your big brother's so cool."
"Thanks. I'm afraid he's taken [spoken for], though."

君の料理は最高だね。
ありがとう、うれしいわ！

"Kimi no ryōri wa saikō da ne."
"Arigatō, ureshii wa!"

"You're a fantastic cook."
"Why, thanks! I'm glad you like it!"

すばらしい成績だ！　よくやった！
僕だってやればできるんだよ。

"Subarashii seiseki da! Yoku yatta!"
"Boku datte yareba dekiru n' da yo."

"These grades are brilliant! Good job!"
"Yeah, once I put my mind to it, I guess I do all right."

あなたって、絵が上手なのね。
ありがとう。子供の頃から、絵は好きだったのよ。

"Anata tte, e ga jōzu na no ne."
"Arigatō. Kodomo no koro kara, e wa suki datta no yo."

"You're quite an artist."
"Thank you. I've enjoyed drawing since I was a child."

あらまあ！　日本語がとってもお上手ですね！
いいえ、とんでもありません。足りないところばかり
です。

"Ara mā! Nihongo ga tottemo ojōzu desu ne!"
"Iie, tonde mo arimasen. Tarinai tokoro bakari desu."

"My, my! You speak such good Japanese!"
"Not at all. I still have so much to learn."

お母様いつもお若いですね。
おかげさまで、元気にしております。

"Okāsama itsumo owakai desu ne."
"Okagesama de, genki ni shite orimasu."

"Your mother always looks so young!"
"Yes, thankfully, she's still in quite good health."

SYMPATHY

Omoiyari 思いやり Thoughtfulness; consideration; kindness marked by sympathy.

➡ あなたにもう少し思いやりがあったら、彼女のつらい立場が分かったはずだ。

Anata ni mō sukoshi omoiyari ga attara, kanojo no tsurai tachiba ga wakatta hazu da.

If you'd been a little more thoughtful, you would have seen what a difficult position she was in.

➡ 私は子供に思いやりのある人に育ってほしい。

Watashi wa kodomo ni omoiyari no aru hito ni sodatte hoshii.

I want my children to grow up to be considerate of others.

Nasake 情け Sympathy; compassion; kindness.

Nasake-bukai 情け深い (Lit., "sympathy is deep") Compassionate; sympathetic; benevolent.

➡ 事故で両親をなくした後、私が温かい家庭で何不自由なく暮らせたのは、情け深い養父母のおかげだ。

Jiko de ryōshin o nakushita ato, watashi ga atatakai katei de nani fu-jiyū naku kuraseta no wa, nasake-bukai yō-fubo no okage da.

I lost my parents in an accident, but I grew up in a good home where I basically had everything I could want, thanks to my foster parents. They were really good to me.

Jō 情 Feelings; emotions; love; affection; sentiment; sympathy.

Jō ni atsui 情に厚い (Lit., "thick with feelings) Extremely empathetic; placing great emphasis on emotional ties.

➡ 彼は情に厚くて親身になって考えてくれるから、困ったことがあれば相談するといいよ。

Kare wa jō ni atsukute shinmi ni natte kangaete kureru kara, komatta koto ga areba sōdan suru to ii yo.

If you're ever in trouble, you should talk to him. He'll put himself in your shoes and do anything he can to help.

Jō ga fukai 情が深い Having deep feelings of affection; caring deeply. (⊗ This term can be used either in a positive sense, or to describe someone whose affection has become a burden for its object.)

➡ 彼女はだれの面倒もよく見るね。情が深いんだね。

Kanojo wa dare no mendō mo yoku miru ne. Jō ga fukai n' da ne.

She's always looking out for everybody. She's really a generous person.

➡ 彼女は情が深すぎて、一緒に暮らしていた男に逃げられてしまった。

Kanojo wa jō ga fukasugite, issho ni kurashite ita otoko ni nigerarete shimatta.

Her love for the man she lived with was so intense that it finally drove him away.

Jō ni hodasareru 情にほだされる (Lit., "be fettered by affection") To take pity on. (⊗ Often used negatively, to describe pity that leads to some complication or trouble.)

A: 「病気の母親をかかえ、仕事もやめてつきっきりで看病しているっていうから、つい情にほだされてなけなしのへそくりをやってしまった」

B: 「でも『情に棹させば流される』っていうよ、ほどほどにしたら？」

A: Byōki no haha o kakae, shigoto mo yamete tsukikkiri de kanbyō shite iru tte iu kara, tsui jō ni hodosarete nakenashi no hesokuri o yatte shimatta.

B: De mo "jō ni saosaseba nagasareru" tte iu yo, hodo-hodo ni shitara?

Person A: He says his mother is sick and he's had to quit his job to take care of her. I couldn't help feeling sorry for him, and gave him what little savings I had."

Person B: Well, you know what they say—pity can be like quicksand. Don't go jumping in too deep."

Mi ni tsumasareru 身につまされる To empathize with someone's situation; to understand all too well how someone feels.

A: 「身につまされるなあ」

B: 「何が？」

A: 「あいつ、仕事、仕事で妻子に逃げられたんだって」

B: 「人ごととは思えないよな、身につまされるよ」

A: Mi ni tsumasareru nā.

B: Nani ga?

A: Aitsu, shigoto, shigoto de saishi ni nigerareta n' da tte.

B: Hitogoto to wa omoenai yo na, mi ni tsumasareru yo.

A: Boy, that hits close to home.

B: What does?

A: That guy, all he thought about was work, work, work—till finally his wife took off with the kids.

B: Yeah, I can relate to that. It does hit home.

Jō ga utsuru 情が移る (Lit., "be infected with feelings) To become attached to; to begin to love. (🖉 This phrase suggests that feelings of love have grown up almost against the speaker's will, over time or because of simple proximity.)

❧ 家に迷い込んできた猫の世話をしているうちに情が移って、とうとう飼うことになってしまった。

Ie ni mayoikonde kita neko no sewa o shite iru uchi ni jō ga utsutte, tōtō kau koto ni natte shimatta.

As I was caring for the stray cat that showed up at our door, I became attached to it and wound up keeping it.

❧ 子供は嫌いだったけれど、妹の子供を預かっているうちに、情が移ってかわいくなった。

Kodomo wa kirai datta keredo, imōto no kodomo o azukatte iru uchi ni, jō ga utsutte kawaiku natta.

I used to hate children, but while I was looking after my sister's kids they started to grow on me.

Chi no kayotta 血の通った (Lit., "blood circulating") Warm; humane.

❧ 幼い子供を置き去りにするなんて、血の通った人間のすることだろうか。

Osanai kodomo o okisari ni suru nante, chi no kayotta ningen no suru koto darō ka.

It's not even human—abandoning a helpless little child.

❧ 社会的弱者のための血の通った政治が望まれる。

Shakai-teki jakusha no tame no chi no kayotta seiji ga nozomareru.

For the sake of society's less fortunate, one can only hope for a more humane government.

Kokoro-zukushi [no] 心尽くし(の) (Lit., "heart-exhausting") Performed with love.

❧ 夫の母は、私たちを心尽くしの手料理でもてなしてくれた。

Otto no haha wa, watashitachi o kokoro-zukushi no ryōri de motenashite kureta.

My husband's mother treated us to a lovingly prepared home-cooked meal.

Tasuke-au 助け合う (Lit., "help together") To help one another out.

➻ 家族は助け合って生きていくものだ。

Kazoku wa tasuke-atte ikite iku mono da.

We have to work together if we're going to be a family.

➻ 同じ町内に住んでいるんですから、仲良く助け合っていきましょうよ。

Onaji chōnai ni sunde iru n' desu kara, naka-yoku tasuke-atte ikimashō yo.

We all live in the same town. Let's try to get along and help each other out.

Hagemasu 励ます To cheer [someone] on in a struggle [to overcome some obstacle].

➻ 彼は瀕死の弟を、救急車が来るまで励まし続けた。

Kare wa hinshi no otōto o, kyūkyū-sha ga kuru made hage-mashitsuzuketa.

He stayed right by his dying brother's side, telling him to hang on, until the ambulance got there.

➻ 私が落ち込んでいるとき、父のことばでどんなに励まされたことか……

Watashi ga ochikonde iru toki, chichi no kotoba de donna ni hagemasareta koto ka ...

I can't tell you how much my father's words lifted me up when I was down.

Yūki-zukeru 勇気づける (Lit., "attach courage") To encourage; to help [someone] find the courage [to do something].

➻ 友人のことばに勇気づけられて、一人で暮らす決心がついた。

Yūjin no kotoba ni yūki-zukerarete, hitori de kurasu kesshin ga tsuita.

My friends were very encouraging, and I decided to move out on my own.

➻ 気持ちが沈んでいるときに、勇気づけてくれる歌もある。

Kimochi ga shizunde iru toki ni, yūkizukete kureru uta mo aru.

There are some songs that can help you keep going when you're feeling low.

Ganbatte 頑張って Hang in there.

➡ A: 「僕たちの交際、両方の親たちに反対されているんだよ」
　 B: 「大変ね、頑張って」

A: Bokutachi no kōsai, ryōhō no oyatachi ni hantai sarete iru n' da yo.
B: Taihen ne, ganbatte.

A: Her folks don't approve of the relationship, and neither do mine.
B: That stinks. Well, don't let it get you down.

Dōjō 同情 (Lit., "same feelings") Sympathy; fellow feeling.

➡ 彼の会社でのつらい立場には同情するよ。

Kare no kaisha de no tsurai tachiba ni wa dōjō suru yo.

I can sympathize with him for the position he's in at the office.

➡ 今回の事件では、犯人に対して同情的な意見が多い。

Konkai no jiken de wa, hannin ni taishite dōjō-teki na iken ga ōi.

A lot of people have expressed sympathy toward the criminal in this case.

➡ 安っぽい同情なんてまっぴらごめんだ。

Yasuppoi dōjō nante mappira gomen da.

I've had enough of your cheap sympathy.
(𝟒 *Mappira gomen* is a set phrase meaning "I've had enough of" or "I'm fed up with.")

Ninjō 人情 (Lit., "people feelings") Human feelings; tenderness; the milk of human kindness.

➡ 私たちの住んでいる所は、人情味あふれる下町です。

Watashitachi no sunde iru tokoro wa, ninjō-mi afureru shita-machi dasu.

We live in the *shitamachi* district, where simple human kindness is a way of life.

➻ 困っている人を見たら、ほうっておけないのが人情だ。

Komatte iru hito o mitara, hōtte okenai no ga ninjō da.

Not being able to turn your back on someone in trouble—that's what *ninjō* is.

Onjō 温情 (Lit., "warm feelings") Mercy; compassion; benevolence.

➻ 裁判官は、罪を深く反省している彼女に温情判決を下した。

Saiban-kan wa, tsumi o fukaku hansei shite iru kanojo ni onjō-hanketsu o kudashita.

Because she showed remorse for her crime, the judge handed down a mercifully light sentence.

➻ 社長の温情主義が裏目に出て、社員たちは仕事を怠けるようになった。

Shachō no onjō-shugi ga urame ni dete, shain-tachi wa shigoto o namakeru yō ni natta.

The president's policy of "benevolent paternalism" backfired on him when the employees began to goof off on the job.

Kōi 好意 Liking; kindness; kind intentions; good will.

➻ 人の好意を踏みにじるようなまねをしてはいけない。

Hito no kōi o fuminijiru yō na mane wa shite wa ikenai.

You shouldn't treat people's kindness as if it meant nothing.

➻ 私たちは、新しい隣人に好意を抱いた。

Watashitachi wa, atarashii rinjin ni kōi o idaita.

We all took a liking to our new neighbor.

Zen'i 善意 Good intentions; a desire to do what is best for someone else.

➻ 人々の善意が、病気の少年を救った。

Hitobito no zen'i ga, byōki no shōnen o sukutta.

People's basic goodness is what saved the sick child.

➼ 本人は善意のつもりでも、他人には迷惑なこともある。

Honnin wa zen'i no tsumori de mo, tanin ni wa meiwaku na koto mo aru.

A person may have the best intentions but still cause trouble for others.

Nagusameru 慰める To comfort someone who's suffered a disappointment; to cheer someone up.

➼ 清美、恋人にふられて落ち込んでるからみんなで慰めようよ。

Kiyomi, koibito ni furarete ochikonde 'ru kara minna de nagusameyō yo.

Kiyomi's depressed because her boyfriend broke up with her. Let's all try to cheer her up.

➼ 慰めのことばなんかいらないよ。

Nagusame no kotoba nanka iranai yo.

I don't need you to comfort me.

Yasashiku suru 優しくする To be nice [kind, good] to someone.

➼ あなたはお姉さんなんだから、弟や妹に優しくしてあげてね。

Anata wa onēsan nan da kara, otōto ya imōto ni yasashiku shite agete ne.

You're the oldest, so be nice to your little brother and sister, OK?

➼ 彼はいつも私に優しくしてくれる。

Kare wa itsumo watashi ni yasashiku shite kureru.

He's always so good to me.

➼ 動物でも優しくしてくれる人は分かって、なつくものだ。

Dōbutsu de mo yasashiku shite kureru hito wa wakatte, natsuku mono da.

Even animals take to people whom they sense will treat them kindly.

Atatakaku mimamoru 温かく見守る (Lit., "warmly

watch over") To watch over someone with an attitude of understanding and tolerance. (𝄞 This phrase is often used in requests. It is a euphemistic way of saying, "Mind your own business and let me do as I please—but be there for me if I get into trouble.")

➻ 若い二人が結婚して新しく家庭を築こうとしています。みんなで温かく見守ってあげましょう。

Wakai futari ga kekkon shite atarashiku katei o kizukō to shite imasu. Minna de atatakaku mimamotte agemashō.

These two young people are going to marry and start a home. Let's give them our support and our best wishes.

➻ 私、彼との交際を宣言します、どうぞ温かく見守ってください。

Watashi, kare to no kōsai o sengen shimasu, dōzo atatakaku mimamotte kudasai.

(Young celebrity): I'd like to announce that he and I are seeing each other. We hope to have your blessings and understanding.

Kokoro no hiroi 心の広い (Lit., "wide-hearted") Kind; compassionate; generous to people in general.

➻ 林先生は、心の広い教師だ。

Hayashi-sensei wa, kokoro no hiroi kyōshi da.

Mr. Hayashi is a teacher with a lot of heart.

➻ 彼女は心の広い人で、私の失敗を許してくれた。

Kanojo wa kokoro no hiroi hito de, watashi no shippai o yurushite kureta.

She's a very nice person, and forgave me for making a mess of things.

Nasake wa hito no tame narazu 情けは人のためならず (Lit., "sympathy is not for others") Your kindness will eventually come back to you; what goes around comes around.

➻ 「彼女は病院でボランティアをしているんだって」

「ふうん、『情けは人のためならず』って言うから、きっと
いいことあるよね」

"Kanojo wa byōin de borantia o shite iru n' datte."
"Fūn, 'nasake wa hito no tame narazu' tte iu kara, kitto ii koto aru yo ne."

"I hear she's doing volunteer work at a hospital."
"Oh yeah? Well, they say what goes around comes around. Now something good will happen to her, you'll see."

➡ 『情けは人のためならず』を『情けをかけるのは、かえっ
てその人のためにならない』と解釈するのは、間違いだ。

'Nasake wa hito no tame narazu' o 'nasake o kakeru no wa, kaette sono hito no tame ni naranai' to kaishaku suru no wa, machigai da.

You've misinterpreted the proverb. *Nasake wa hito no tame narazu* doesn't mean that there's no point in showing compassion for a person.

FRIENDS AND NEIGHBORS

Yūjō 友情 Friendship; feelings of love [affection] between friends.

➡ 彼と僕とは、固い友情で結ばれている。

Kare to boku to wa, katai yūjō de musubarete iru.

He and I are very tight friends.

➡ 私たちは学生時代の友情を今でも大切にしている。

Watashitachi wa gakusei-jidai no yūjō o ima de mo taisetsu ni shite iru.

The friendship we shared as students is still important to us today.

Tomodachi/yūjin 友達/友人 A friend; friends. (❧ The terms *tomodachi* and *yūjin* are nearly identical, but *tomodachi*, pronounced with the Japanese reading, is a little more casual. Japanese men, in particular, may tend to substitute the term *yūjin* for *tomodachi* when talking with people in more formal settings.)

⇴ 彼女は性格が明るくて、友達も多い。

Kanojo wa seikaku ga akarukute, tomodachi mo ōi.

She's a cheerful, outgoing girl with lots of friends.

⇴ 彼は私の大切な友人だ。

Kare wa watashi no taisetsu na yūjin da.

He's a close friend of mine.

⇴ 友達を裏切ってはいけない。

Tomodachi o uragitte wa ikenai.

You must never betray a friend.

⇴ ずっと友達でいましょう。

Zutto tomodachi de imashō.

Let's always be friends.

Nakayoshi/naka ga ii 仲良し/仲がいい (Lit., "good relations/relations are good") Friends; pals; close/being friends; being close; being on good terms.

⇴ うちの子と竜ちゃんは幼稚園の仲良しだ。

Uchi no ko to Ryū-chan wa yōchi-en no nakayoshi da.

Ryu-chan and our daughter are best pals in kindergarten.

⇴ あなたは、姉と仲良しだった木村さんじゃありませんか。

Anata wa, ane to nakayoshi datta Kimura-san ja arimasen ka.

You're Ms. Kimura, aren't you? You were good friends with my sister.

⇴ きみたち夫婦ってほんとうにいつも仲がいいね。

Kimitachi fūfu tte hontō ni itsumo naka ga ii ne.

(Said to a couple): You guys always seem to get along so well.

(⚓ Reversing the word order here of *naka ga ii* to *ii naka [desu]* gives yet another meaning: to be involved in a sexual [romantic] relationship; to have a thing going.)

Nakanaori suru 仲直りする (Lit., "fixing relations") To make up with [someone after a quarrel].

➡ 今日は花でも買って帰って奥さんと仲直りしたら？

Kyō wa hana de mo katte kaette okusan to nakanaori shi-tara?

Why don't you make up with your wife? Get her some flowers or something on your way home.

Osananajimi 幼なじみ Friends since childhood; a friend one has known since childhood.

➡ キースは幼なじみのアンと結婚した。

Kiisu wa osananajimi no An to kekkon shita.

Keith married Ann, whom he'd known since childhood.

➡ A: 「真紀ちゃんとつき合ってるんだって？」
　 B: 「まさか！　単なる幼なじみだよ」

A: Maki-chan to tsukiatte 'ru n' datte?
B: Masaka! Tannaru osananajimi da yo.

A: Is it true you're going out with Maki?
B: Hell no! She and I have been friends since we were kids, that's all.

Chikuba no tomo 竹馬の友 (Lit., "stilts friends") A childhood friend or playmate (with whom you go so far back that you might once have played on stilts together).

➡ 彼と首相は竹馬の友だ。

Kare to shushō wa chikuba no tomo da.

He and the prime minister have been friends since childhood.

Ki ga au/uma ga au 気が合う/馬が合う (Lit., "the *ki* matches/the horse matches") To get along well with; to be compatible with.

➡ A: 「あの二人いつも一緒にいるけどよっぽど気が合うんだね」
　 B: 「相性がいいって言うのかな？」

A: *Ano futari itsumo issho ni iru kedo yoppodo ki ga au n' da ne.*

B: *Aishō ga ii tte iu no ka na?*

A: Those two are always together. They seem to get along pretty well.

B: Yeah, they must be pretty compatible.

➥ 彼女のことなんとなく苦手なの。馬が合わないのかも……

Kanojo no koto nanto naku nigate na no. Uma ga awanai no ka mo ...

I have some trouble with her. I guess we just don't get along ...

Au 合う To hit it off; to get along well.

➥ 彼とは、初めてのデートだったの。でも私とは合わないみたい……

Kare to wa, hajimete no dēto datta no. Demo watashi to wa awanai mitai ...

It was only our first date but we didn't really hit it off.

Yūai 友愛 Affection for a friend; friendship.

➥ 彼の弔辞は友愛にあふれ、参列者の胸を打つものだった。

Kare no chōji wa yūai ni afure, sanretsu-sha no mune o utsu mono datta.

The mourners were all moved by the speech he gave at the memorial service, filled as it was with affection for his friend.

➥ 赤十字の活動は、友愛・奉仕の精神に基づいている。

Seki-jūji no katsudō wa, yūai-hōshi no seishin ni motozuite iru.

The work of the Red Cross is rooted in a spirit of friendship and [community] service.

Kyūkō o atatameru 旧交を温める To renew an old friendship; pick a friendship up where you left off.

➥ 私たちはクラス会で久しぶりに旧交を温めた。

Watashitachi wa kurasu-kai de hisashi-buri ni kyūkō o atatameta.

After all these years, we renewed our friendship at the class reunion.

Rinjin-ai 隣人愛 (Lit., "neighbor love") Neighborly good will; a spirit of cooperation among neighbors.

➡ 震災のおかげで、被災地の人々の間には隣人愛が生まれた。

Shinsai no okage de hisai-chi no hitobito no aida ni wa rinjin-ai ga umareta.

As a result of the earthquake, a spirit of neighborly good will grew up in the affected area.

Jinrui-ai 人類愛 (Lit., "human race love") Love for all people, regardless of race, nationality, or creed.

➡ 飢餓に苦しんでいる人たちに援助の手を差し伸べようという、人類愛に基づいた活動がもっと盛んになればいい。

Kiga ni kurushinde iru hitotachi ni enjo no te o sashinobeyō to iu, jinrui-ai ni motozuita katsudō ga motto sakan ni nareba ii.

The campaign to help people suffering from starvation is based on love for all mankind. I hope to see it gain momentum.

Haku-ai 博愛 Philanthropy; charity; love of mankind; fraternity

➡ クリミア戦争のとき、ナイチンゲールは博愛の精神で敵の傷病兵も救った。

Kurimia sensō no toki, Naichingēru wa haku-ai no seishin de teki no shōbyō-hei mo sukutta.

During the Crimean War, Florence Nightingale showed her love for all mankind by helping even enemy soldiers who were sick and wounded.

➡ フランスの国旗の三色は、自由・平等・博愛を表している。

Fransu no kokki no sanshoku wa, jiyū-byōdō-haku-ai o arawashite iru.

The three colors of the French flag stand for liberty, equality, and fraternity.

Nanji no teki o aise yo 汝の敵を愛せよ Love thine enemy. (✌ Many phrases from the Bible are well known and commonly used in Japan, even by non-Christians.)

➾ A: 「もういいかげんに許してやれよ、聖書にも『汝の敵を愛せよ』ってあるじゃないか」
B: 「冗談じゃないよ、敵は憎らしいもんよ」

A: Mō ii kagen ni yurushite yare yo, seisho ni mo "nanji no teki o aise yo" tte aru ja nai ka.
B: Jōdan ja nai yo, teki wa nikurashii mon yo.

A: You've been holding this grudge long enough. Why don't you forgive the guy? You know, like it says in the Bible and all, "Love thine enemy."
B: Don't be ridiculous. I hate my enemies.

Keiai 敬愛 Respect and affection; admiration

➾ 今日は、敬愛する恩師の古希のお祝いがあります。

Kyō wa, keiai suru onshi no koki no oiwai ga arimasu.

Today there's a party to celebrate the seventieth birthday of a teacher for whom I have great respect and affection.

➾ 彼女は、名付け親のおじいさんに敬愛の気持ちを抱いている。

Kanojo wa, nazuke-oya no ojiisan ni keiai no kimochi o idaite iru.

She has the highest regard for her elderly godfather.

Shin'ai 親愛 Intimacy; close friendship; affection. (✌ This word is usually used in one of two fixed phrases: *shin'ai no jō* ["a token of friendship"] and the formal term *shin'ai-naru*, often used in letter writing, meaning "dear" or "beloved.")

➾ 彼は妹の夫となる青年に、ゴルフのクラブを贈って親愛の情を示した。

Kare wa imōto no otto to naru seinen ni, gorufu no kurabu o okutte shinai no jō o shimeshita.

He sent his younger sister's fiancé a set of golf clubs, as a token of their friendship.

➡ A: 「痛いな！　ひとの背中を叩くなよ！」
　　B: 「いいじゃないか、親愛の情だよ」

　A: Itai na! Hito no senaka o tataku na yo!
　B: Ii ja nai ka, shin'ai no jō da yo.

　A: Ow! Don't pound on my back like that!
　B: Oh, come on. It's just a way of expressing friendship.

Sonkei suru　尊敬する　To respect.

➡ A: 「私、尊敬できない相手とは、結婚できないの」
　　B: 「私、あなたと付き合っている彼、尊敬しちゃうけど」

　A: Watashi, sonkei dekinai aite to wa, kekkon dekinai no.
　B: Watashi, anata to tsukiatte iru kare, sonkei shichau kedo.

　A: I could never marry anyone I didn't respect.
　B: Well, I gotta respect the guy who's going out with you.

➡ 私は学問に一生を捧げた祖父を尊敬している。

　Watashi wa gakumon ni isshō o sasageta sofu o sonkei shite iru.

　I respect my grandfather, who devoted his whole life to his studies.

➡ 彼の勇気ある行動は尊敬に値する。

　Kare no yūki aru kōdō wa sonkei ni atai suru.

　His courageous deeds are worthy of respect.

Kenshin　献身　(Lit., "donate body") Self-sacrifice; unselfish devotion to a person or cause. (⚐ This phrase is almost always used in the adjectival, ~-teki, construction, rather than alone as a noun.)

➡ マザー・テレサは恵まれない人々に献身的につくした。

　Mazā Teresa wa megumarenai hitobito ni kenshin-teki ni tsukushita.

　Mother Teresa has devoted her life to helping the disadvantaged.

●● 夫の献身的な看護で、彼女は回復していった。

Otto no kenshin-teki na kango de, kanojo wa kaifuku shite itta.

With her husband dedicating himself body and soul to her care, she gradually got better and better.

Chūjitsu na 忠実な Faithful; loyal; true.

●● A: 「宏ったら、ジュディーのこと必ず門のところで待っているのよ」

  B: 「ふうん、忠実な犬みたいね」

  A: Hiroshi ttara, Judii no koto kanarazu mon no tokoro de matte iru no yo.

  B: Fūn, chūjitsu na inu mitai ne.

  A: That Hiroshi. He never fails to be waiting at the gate for Judy.

  B: Hmph. Like a faithful dog, eh?

●● 忠実なメイドは、主人の行動を逐一奥様に報告した。

Chūjitsu na meido wa, shujin no kōdō o chikuichi okusama ni hōkoku shita.

The wife's loyal maid reported every move the husband made.

Borantia ボランティア Volunteer [charity] work; also, one engaged in such work.

●● 学生たちの間でもボランティア活動は盛んになってきている。

Gakusei-tachi no aida de mo borantia katsudō wa sakan ni natte kite iru.

Volunteer work is getting more popular with students these days.

●● おかあさんは週に2回、病院にボランティアに行っている。

Okāsan wa shū ni nikai, byōin ni borantia ni itte iru.

My mother goes to a hospital twice a week to do charity work.

●● 妻は僕に「あなたと結婚したのは、ボランティア精神からよ」なんて言うんだ。

Tsuma wa boku ni "anata to kekkon shita no wa, borantia-seishin kara yo" nante iu n' da.

My wife tells me she only married me out of charity.

HIGHER LOVE

Jihi 慈悲 Compassion; mercy; the compassion of Buddha and the bodhisattvas for all living beings.

➥ 慈悲深いその老紳士は、長い間ユニセフに多額の寄付を続けた。

Jihi-bukai sono rō-shinshi wa, nagai aida yunisefu ni tagaku no kifu o tsuzuketa.

That compassionate old gentleman regularly donated large sums to UNICEF.

Kago 加護 Divine protection.

➥ クリスチャンの母は、私たち兄弟がたいした病気もせずに大きくなったことを、神のご加護があったからだと信じている。

Kurisuchan no haha wa, watashitachi kyōdai ga taishita byōki mo sezu ni ōkiku natta koto o, kami no gokago ga atta kara da to shinjite iru.

My Christian mother believes that the reason my brothers and sisters and I grew up without ever having any serious illnesses is that God was protecting us.

➥ あなたに神のご加護がありますように。

Anata ni kami no gokago ga arimasu yō ni.

May God be with you.

(⚑ This phrase is from the Japanese Mass.)

THANKFULNESS

On ni kiru 恩に着る To be deeply grateful for a favor; to feel oneself indebted.

➡ あのとき失敗をかばってくれた上司には今でも恩に着ているんですよ。

Ano toki shippai o kabatte kureta jōshi ni wa ima de mo on ni kite iru n' desu yo.

I'm still extremely grateful to my supervisor for covering for me when I made that mistake.

➡ 弟：「お願い、必ず返すから一万円貸してよ。彼女がデートをOKしてくれたんだ」
　姉：「しょうがないわねえ、ちゃんと返してよ」
　弟：「ありがとう、恩に着るよ」

Otōto:　Onegai, kanarazu kaesu kara ichiman-en kashite yo. Kanojo ga dēto o ōkē shite kureta n' da.

Ane:　　Shō ga nai wa nē, chanto kaeshite yo.

Otōto:　Arigatō, on ni kiru yo.

Brother:　　Please. I promise I'll pay you back, so lend me 10,000 yen. She [finally] agreed to go out with me.

Older sister:　Oh, all right, but make sure you return it.

Brother:　　Thanks. I'll never forget this.

Kansha suru 感謝する To be grateful.

➡ A：「この舞台のチケット、手に入れるの大変だったんだから」
　B：「分かってるって、感謝してるよ」

A:　Kono butai no chiketto, te ni ireru no taihen datta n' da kara.

B:　Wakatte 'ru tte, kansha shite 'ru yo.

A:　Hey, these theater tickets were really hard to get, you know.

B:　I know that. And I'm grateful, don't worry.

➡ 彼らは毎日、神への感謝の祈りを欠かさない。

Karera wa mainichi, kami e no kansha no inori o kakasanai.

Each day, without fail, they offer prayers of thanks to God.

Ashi o mukete nerarenai 足を向けて寝られない (Lit., "can't sleep with one's feet pointed toward") To "owe" someone; to be eternally grateful.

➥ あの先生は私の命を救ってくれたの。足を向けて寝られな
いわ。

*Ano sensei wa watashi no inochi o sukutte kureta no. Ashi
o mukete nerarenai wa.*

That doctor saved my life. I'll always be grateful to him.

BELOVED THINGS

Gusai 愚妻 (Lit., "stupid wife") My wife; my old lady (⚜
The tone of deprecation here actually suggests intimacy
and fondness.)

➥ A:「君のセーターいいね。奥さんの手製？」
　 B:「いやあ、お恥ずかしい。愚妻は暇なもんで、こんなこ
　　　とばかりやっているんですよ」

　 A: *Kimi no sētā ii ne. Okusan no tesei?*
　 B: *Iyā, ohazukashii. Gusai wa hima na mon de, konna koto
　　　bakari yatte iru n' desu yo.*

　 A: That's a nice sweater! Did your wife make it for you?
　 B: Yeah, I'm afraid so. She's got to do something to fill up
　　　her time, so she's always making stuff like this.

Uchi no yatsu うちのやつ (Lit., "guy in my house") My
wife. (⚜ This term too is only superficially deprecatory.)

➥ A:「うちのやつ、カルチャーセンターだとかいって出てば
　　　かりいるんだよ」
　 B:「うちのやつだって！」

　 A: *Uchi no yatsu, karuchā sentā da to ka itte dete bakari
　　　iru n' da yo.*
　 B: *Uchi no yatsu datte!*

　 A: My wife's never home, she's always running off to the
　　　culture center or some damn place.
　 B: Same here!

Teishu 亭主 (Lit., "master") My husband; my old man.
(⚜ The nuance here is familiar and comfortable.)

➡ A:「うちの亭主、休みっていうとごろごろして、文句ばか
　　り……」

　B:「あら、お宅のご主人、愛妻家という評判よ」

　A: *Uchi no teishu, yasumi tte iu to gorogoro shite, monku
　　bakari …*

　B: *Ara, otaku no go-shujin, aisai-ka to iu hyōban yo.*

　A: On his days off, my husband just lies around the house,
　　complaining …

　B: Really? Everyone thinks of him as a very loving hus-
　　band.

Manamusume 愛娘 One's [darling] daughter. (⚠ Used only in reference to someone else's daughter.)

➡ 彼は愛娘のために、ボーナスでピアノを買った。

Kare wa manamusume no tame ni, bōnasu de piano o katta.

With his bonus, he bought his darling daughter a piano.

➡ 彼は愛娘にボーイフレンドができたのがおもしろくないよ
うだ。

*Kare wa manamusume ni bōifurendo ga dekita no ga omo-
shirokunai yō da.*

He doesn't seem too thrilled about his baby girl having gotten herself a boyfriend.

Aisoku 愛息 One's [beloved] son. (⚠ Used only in refer-ence to someone else's son.)

➡ 彼の愛息は、病院を継がせたいという父親の期待にそむい
て文学を志した。

*Kare no aisoku wa, byōin o tsugasetai to iu chichi-oya no
kitai ni somuite bungaku o kokorozashita.*

He'd hoped that his beloved son would take over his med-
ical clinic one day, but the kid let him down by pursuing
literature.

Itoshigo 愛し子 One's [beloved] baby [small child]. (⚠ Used only in reference to someone else's child.)

➡ 彼女はたった一人の愛し子を家事で失ってしまった。

Kanojo wa tatta hitori no itoshigo o kaji de ushinatte shi-matta.

She lost her beloved only child in the fire.

Manadeshi 愛弟子 A favorite pupil or apprentice.

•• 彼女はかのルーヴィンシュタインの愛弟子だ。

Kanojo wa kano Rūbinshutain no manadeshi da.

She's a protegée of the great Rubinstein.

•• 彼は愛弟子の出世を誰よりも喜んだ。

Kare wa manadeshi no shusse o dare yori mo yorokonda.

He was more delighted than anyone by his favorite pupil's success.

Aigan 愛玩 Prized; pet.

•• 最近は、爬虫類を愛玩する人もいるそうだ。

Saikin wa, hachū-rui o aigan suru hito mo iru sō da.

I hear that some people like to keep reptiles as pets these days.

•• 愛玩動物を飼うことは、老人や病人の慰めになる。

Aigan-dōbutsu o kau koto wa, rōjin ya byōnin no nagusame ni naru.

Having a pet can be a comfort to people who are elderly or sickly.

Aiken 愛犬 One's [beloved] dog.

•• 彼の愛犬が死んでから、もう2年になる。

Kare no aiken ga shinde kara, mō ninen ni naru.

It's been two years since his [faithful old] dog died.

Aibyō 愛猫 One's [beloved] cat.

•• わが家の愛猫は、メイという名の黒猫です。

Wagaya no aibyō wa, Mei to iu na no kuroneko desu.

Our kitty is a [beautiful] black one named May.

Aidoku-sho 愛読書 A favorite book; a book one likes well enough to read and reread.

➡ 私の愛読書は、川端康成の『雪国』だ。

Watashi no aidoku-sho wa, Kawabata Yasunari no "Yuki-guni" da.

My favorite book is Yasunari Kawabata's *Snow Country*.

Aikoku-shin 愛国心 Patriotism; love of one's country.

➡ A: 「近頃の日本人は愛国心に欠けている、なんて言われるけれど、そうでもないんじゃない？」

B: 「特に、オリンピックのときなんかね」

A: Chikagoro no nihon-jin wa aikoku-shin ni kakete iru, nante iwareru keredo, sō de mo nai n' ja nai?

B: Tokuni, Orinpikku no toki nanka ne.

A: They say Japanese are lacking in patriotism these days, but I don't think that's true. Do you?

B: No. Especially, like, during the Olympics.

Aiyō suru 愛用する To use a favorite object or device frequently.

➡ あなたにもらった辞書は、とても使いやすくて、いまでも愛用しています。

Anata ni moratta jisho wa, totemo tsukai-yasukute, ima de mo aiyō shite imasu.

That dictionary you gave me is really easy to use, and it still comes in handy.

Aichaku 愛着 (Lit., "love sticks") Attachment; affection.

➡ このカバンはもう傷んでしまって外へは持って行けないが、愛着があって捨てられない。

Kono kaban wa mō itande shimatte soto e wa motte ikenai ga, aichaku ga atte suterarenai.

This briefcase is so beat up I can't carry it in public, yet I'm too attached to it to throw it out.

Aisha 愛車 One's car or vehicle.

➡ 鈴木さんの愛車はV-マックスですよね。

Suzuki-san no aisha wa Bui-makkusu desu yo ne.

You drive a V-Max, don't you, Mr. Suzuki?

PARENTS AND CHILDREN

Bosei-ai 母性愛 Maternal love; a mother's [instinctual] love for her children.

➡ 身を挺してひなを守る親鳥を見ていると、下手な人間の親より母性愛が強いような気さえする。

Mi o teishite hina o mamoru oyadori o mite iru to, heta na ningen no oya yori bosei-ai ga tsuyoi yō na ki sae suru.

When you watch a mother bird risking her life to protect her babies, you wonder if the maternal instinct isn't stronger in them than in some human mothers.

➡ 小犬を見てかわいいと思うのも簿性愛かしら？

Ko-inu o mite kawaii to omou no mo bosei-ai kashira?

When you see a little puppy and think "oh, how cute," could that be called a maternal instinct, I wonder?

Fusei-ai 父性愛 Paternal love; a father's love for his children.

➡ 彼女の花嫁姿に父親が見せた涙は、父性愛の表れとして私の胸を打った。

Kanojo no hanayome-sugata ni chichi-oya ga miseta namida wa, fusei-ai no araware to shite watashi no mune o utta.

I was touched by the love evident in her father's tears as he gazed at her in her wedding gown.

Oyagokoro 親心 (Lit., "parent heart") The love of a parent for a child.

➡ 彼は娘が結婚するとき、「つらかったらいつでも帰っておいで」って言ったんだって。親心だね。

Kare wa musume ga kekkon suru toki, "Tsurakattara itsu-

demo kaette oide" tte itta n' datte. Oyagokoro da ne.

When she got married, her father told her to feel free to come back home any time if things got rough. That's *oya-gokoro*.

➡ おとうさん、私のこと心配してくれるのは親心だって分かるんだけど、私だってもう立派な大人なのよ。

Otōsan, watashi no koto shinpai shite kureru no wa oya-gokoro datte wakaru n' da kedo, watashi datte mō rippa na otona na no yo.

I understand you're my father and you care about me and that's why you worry so much, but I'm a big girl [an adult] now.

Oyaomoi 親思い (Lit., "parent thoughts") A person who loves and is considerate of his or her parents.

➡ 次男は親思いで、毎晩必ず電話をかけてきて体の具合を気づかってくれる。

Jinan wa oyaomoi de, maiban kanarazu denwa o kakete kite karada no guai o kizukatte kureru.

Our second son is a really thoughtful boy. He calls every night to ask how we're feeling.

➡ 隣の息子は親思いで評判だ。

Tonari no musuko wa oyaomoi de hyōban da.

Everyone considers the young man next door a model son to his parents.

Oya-kōkō 親孝行 Filial piety; taking good care of one's parents.

➡ 心配をかけないのが一番の親孝行だ。

Shinpai o kakenai no ga ichiban no oya-kōkō da.

The best way to be a good son [daughter] to your parents is not to give them any cause for worry.

➡ 「親孝行したいときには親はなし」って、本当だね。

"Oya-kōkō shitai toki ni wa oya wa nashi" tte, hontō da ne.

"When you finally decide to do right by your parents, it's often too late"—how true!

Ko-bonnō 子煩悩 (Lit., "child passion") Having an exceptionally strong love for one's children; also, one who has such a love.

❧ 夫は子煩悩で、疲れていても子供の宿題をみてやったり一緒にゲームをしたりする。

Otto wa ko-bonnō de, tsukarete ite mo kodomo no shukudai o mite yattari issho ni gēmu o shitari suru.

My husband's crazy about the kids. Even when he's tired, he takes time to look over their homework or play some game with them.

❧ 彼は子煩悩というよりはむしろ親ばかだ。

Kare wa ko-bonnō to iu yori wa mushiro oyabaka da.

He doesn't just *love* his children—he's a complete fool when it comes to them.

Ko wa kasugai 子はかすがい (Lit., "child is a clamp") Having a child will keep a couple together even when they don't get along.

❧ 彼女たち、離婚するのはやめたらしいよ。やっぱり子はかすがいなんだね。

Kanojo-tachi, rikon suru no wa yameta rashii yo. Yappari ko wa kasugai nan da ne.

Apparently she and her husband decided not to divorce. It's like they say, children *do* keep you together.

❧ 子はかすがいかもしれないけれど、悩みの種でもあるんだよね。

Ko wa kasugai ka mo shirenai keredo, nayami no tane de mo aru n' da yo ne.

Children may be a tie that binds, but they're also a constant source of worry.

Ai no kesshō 愛の結晶 (Lit., "crystal of love") The fruit of a [married] couple's union; a child.

➡ ご結婚おめでとうございます。次はいよいよ愛の結晶ですね。

Go-kekkon omedetō gozaimasu. Tsugi wa iyo-iyo ai no kessho desu ne.

Congratulations on your marriage. Now you just need to start filling up the nest with little ones.

Honobono to shita ほのぼのとした Heartwarming.

➡ あの二人を見ていると、こちらまでほのぼのとした気分になってくる。

Ano futari o mite iru to, kochira made honobono to shita kibun ni natte kuru.

Just watching those two makes you feel all warm and fuzzy inside.

➡ 裕福ではないけれど、家族が信頼しあって生きているあの若い一家には、ほのぼのとしたものを感じる。

Yūfuku de wa nai keredo, kazoku ga shinrai shiatte ikite iru ano wakai ikka ni wa, honobono to shita mono o kanjiru.

They may not be rich, but it sure is nice to see how the members of that young family pull together and help each other out all the time.

Itooshii いとおしい Dearly loved.

➡ 腕の中で眠ってしまった子供の寝顔を見ていると、いとおしくて胸がジーンと熱くなる。

Ude no naka de nemutte shimatta kodomo no negao o mite iru to, itōshikute mune ga jiin to atsuku naru.

When the baby's sleeping in my arms and I look down at her sweet little face, it just gets me right here [putting a hand to one's breast].

Itsukushimu いつくしむ To love; to care for tenderly.

➡ 私たち兄弟は両親にいつくしみながら育てられ、幸せな子供時代を過ごした。

Watashitachi kyōdai wa ryōshin ni itsukushiminagara so-daterare, shiawase na kodomo-jidai o sugoshita.

Our mother and father gave us plenty of love when we were growing up, and we all had happy childhoods.

➡ 彼は私をいつくしむように、優しく見つめた。

Kare wa watashi o itsukushimu yō ni, yasashiku mitsumeta.

He gazed at me tenderly, as if he truly loved me.

Oyabaka 親馬鹿 To love a child so much that one loses all perspective; also, the parent who does so; a doting parent.

➡ A:（新生児室で）「ほら見て！　やっぱりうちの子がいちばん美人よ」

B:「生まれたばかりなんて、みんな同じよ。もう親馬鹿になっちゃって！」

A: (shinseiji-shitsu de) Hora mite! Yappari uchi no ko ga ichiban bijin yo.

B: Umareta bakari nante, minna onaji yo. Mō oyabaka ni nachatte!

Mother A:　(in the nursery) Look! Our little girl's the prettiest of them all!

Mother B:　Newborns all look alike. You've already lost all objectivity!

➡ 親馬鹿チャンリン（そばやの風鈴）

Oyabaka-chanrin (soba-ya no fūrin)

(Lit., "Doting parent, ding-dong [wind chimes of soba shop]") A nonsensical, singsong set phrase used to tease a doting parent. *Chanrin* is onomatopoeic for the sound of wind chimes hanging outside a soba shop.

Oya no yokume 親の欲目 A parent's partiality [bias]; overestimation of one's own child's talent, looks, etc.

➡ 親の欲目か、うちの子が一番美人に見える。

Oya no yokume ka, uchi no ko ga ichiban bijin ni mieru.

Perhaps I'm biased, but our little girl looks prettier to me than all the rest.

➡ A:「うちの子、生き物が好きだから、将来はきっと生物学者だな」

B: 「親の欲目だろ。そんなに頭がよさそうにも思えないぜ」

A: *Uchi no ko, ikimono ga suki dakara, shōrai wa kitto seibutsu-gakusha da na.*

B: *Oya no yokume daro. Sonna ni atama ga yosa sō ni mo omoenai ze.*

A: Our son likes animals. I'm sure he'll be a biologist when he grows up.

B: Uh-huh, right. You really think he looks that smart, do you?

Amaeru 甘える To depend on a person for love and affection; to want to be babied.

➻ 私、彼に甘えてばっかり。

Watashi, kare ni amaete bakkari.

Without him, I just don't know what I'd do!

➻ 上の子は自立心が強くて何でも自分でやろうとするが、下の子は自分でできることでも親に甘えてやってもらおうとする。

Ue no ko wa jiritsu-shin ga tsuyokute nandemo jibun de yarō to suru ga, shita no ko wa jibun de dekiru koto de mo oya ni amaete yatte moraō to suru.

Our older child is very independent and tries to do everything by herself, but the younger one just wants us to baby him.

➻ 彼女は末っ子で甘やかされて育った。

Kanojo wa suekko de amayakasarete sodatta.

As the youngest child, she was always pampered by her parents.

➻ あの子は、ママの後ばかりついて歩いて、ほんとうに甘えっ子だね。

Ano ko wa, mama no ato bakari tsuite aruite, hontō ni amaekko da ne.

That kid is always hanging on his mother's skirt. What a mama's boy.

Me o hosomeru/me o hosoku suru 目を細める/目を細

くする (Lit., "narrow one's eyes") To beam with pleasure.

➨ 彼は、6か月の娘がやっとハイハイできるようになったといって、目を細めた。

Kare wa, rokkagetsu no musume ga yatto haihai dekiru yō ni natta to itte, me o hosometa.

He beamed with joy as he told us that his six-month-old daughter had started to crawl.

➨ おばあちゃんは好物のようかんに目を細めている。

Obāchan wa kōbutsu no yōkan ni me o hosomete iru.

Grandmother smiled with anticipation at the sight of the sweet bean jelly she's so fond of.

Sōgō o kuzusu 相好を崩す (Lit., "demolish one's face) To smile with delight; to be all smiles.

➨ 父は私の息子をひざに乗せて相好を崩している。

Chichi wa watashi no musuko o hiza ni nosete sōgō o kuzushite iru.

Dad's all smiles as he sits there holding my son on his lap.

Me no naka ni irete mo itakunai 目の中に入れても痛くない (Lit., "even putting [someone] right into one's eye wouldn't hurt") A set phrase declaring that someone is completely taken with someone else (usually used when children are the objects of love).

➨ 夫は一番下の娘を、目の中に入れても痛くないほどかわいがっている。

Otto wa ichiban shita no musume o, me no naka ni irete mo itakunai hodo kawaigatte iru.

My husband just goes gaga over our youngest daughter.

➨ あんなに子供なんか嫌いだって言っていたのに、変わるもんだねえ、君が、坊やを見る目ときたら「もう、目の中に入れても痛くない」って感じだよ。

Anna ni kodomo nanka kirai da tte itte ita no ni, kawaru mon' da nē, kimi ga, bōya o miru me to kitara "mō, me no naka ni iretemo itakunai" tte kanji da yo.

To think you used to say you hated children. You sure have changed. When you look at your son, it's as if you could eat him right up.

Tabete shimaitai kurai 食べてしまいたいくらい (Lit., "One would practically like to eat [someone] up") (❦ Similar to the previous entry, but can be used more widely, including with regard to potential lovers.)

◦◦ 君のこと大好き！　もう食べてしまいたい！

Kimi no koto daisuki! Mō tabete shimaitai!

I'm crazy about you! I could just eat you right up!

◦◦ 赤ちゃんのあどけないしぐさを見ていると、いとおしくて食べてしまいたいくらいだ。

Akachan no adokenai shigusa o miteiru to, itōshikute tabete shimaitai kurai da.

When I'm watching my baby's innocent little gestures, he's so adorable I could just eat him right up.

Teshio ni kakete sodateru 手塩にかけて育てる (Lit., "raise by treating with salt") To raise [a child] with painstaking care and a hands-on approach.

◦◦ 両親は私を手塩にかけて育ててくれた。

Ryōshin wa watashi o teshio ni kakete sodatete kureta.

My parents were always there for me as I was growing up.

◦◦ 手塩にかけて育てたランナーの初勝利に、監督は目をうるませた。

Teshio ni kakete sodateta rannā no hatsu-shōri ni, kantoku wa me o urumaseta.

The coach's eyes misted up when the runner he'd devoted so much care to training won his first race.

Kabau かばう To shelter or protect [someone] from harm; to cover for.

◦◦ 兄は私をかばって、花瓶を割ったのは自分だと嘘をついた。

Ani wa watashi o kabatte, kabin o watta no wa jibun da to uso o tsuita.

My brother covered for me by lying and saying he was the one who'd broken the vase.

➮ いつまでも親がかばってくれると思ったら、大きな間違いだ。

Itsumademo oya ga kabatte kureru to omottara, ōmachigai da.

If you think your parents are going to look out for you forever, you've got another think coming.

➮ 痛めた右足をかばって歩いたために、左の腰が痛い。

Itameta migiashi o kabatte aruita tame ni, hidari no koshi ga itai.

My left hip hurts because I was favoring my injured right foot when I walked.

Mamoru 守る/護る To protect; to defend; to watch over.

➮ 「あなたのことは一生全力でお守りします」なんて、誰か言ってくれないかなあ。

"Anata no koto wa isshō zenryoku de omamori shimasu" nante, dare ka itte kurenai ka nā.

"I'll do my best to protect and defend you as long as I live." How I wish someone would say that to me!
(☙ These are the exact words that the Crown Prince used in proposing to Crown Princess Masako. This phrase is very well known, for that reason, in Japan.)

➮ 私たちは野鳥を守る運動をしている。

Watashitachi wa yachō o mamoru undō o shite iru.

We are involved in a movement to protect wild birds.

Me o kakeru 目をかける To look after; to take care of; to look out for [someone's] well-being.

➮ 私が長年目をかけてきた教え子なので、彼の受賞は自分のことのようにうれしい。

Watashi ga naganen me o kakete kita oshiego na no de, kare no jushō wa jibun no koto no yō ni ureshii.

I watched him develop over the course of many years when he was my student, so I was as thrilled when he won the award as if I had won it myself.

➨ 大家の老婦人はうちの子供たちに、なにかと目をかけてくれる。

Ōya no rō-fujin wa uchi no kodomo-tachi ni, nanika to me o kakete kureru.

Our elderly landlady looks after the children in various ways.

Kage ni nari hinata ni nari 陰になり日向になり (Lit., "being [one's] shade, being [one's] sunshine") To always be there for [someone], through thick and thin.

➨ 姉は私のことを陰になり日向になり支えてくれた。

Ane wa watashi no koto o kage ni nari hinata ni nari sasaete kureta.

My sister was always there for me, no matter what.

Onba-higasa 乳母日傘 (Lit., "wet nurse and parasol") A wealthy family's pampered child. (⚯ This is a set phrase, somewhat similar, perhaps, to being "born with a silver spoon in one's mouth.")

➨ 旧家の令嬢として乳母日傘で育てられた直美は、いまだに一人で電車に乗ったことがない。

Kyūka no reijō to shite onba-higasa de sodaterareta Naomi wa, imada ni hitori de densha ni notta koto ga nai.

Raised as the pampered daughter of an aristocratic family, to this day Naomi has never boarded a train alone.

Chō yo hana yo 蝶よ花よ (Lit., "A butterfly! A flower!") Similar to the previous entry, refers to an upbringing in which the child [usually daughter] is treated as tenderly as a butterfly or a flower.

➨ 彼女は裕福な商家の一人娘で、蝶よ花よと育てられた。

Kanojo wa yūfuku na shōka no hitori-musume de, chō yo hana yo to sodaterareta.

Being the only daughter of a wealthy merchant, she was

treated like some precious, fragile flower.

Hakoiri-musume 箱入り娘 (Lit., "daughter in a box") A young woman who has always been protected from the harsh realities of life by doting parents.

➡ 彼女は箱入り娘で、箸より重いものを持ったことがない。

Kanojo wa hakoiri-musume de, hashi yori omoi mono o motta koto ga nai.

She grew up in a sheltered environment—she's never lifted anything heavier than a chopstick.

➡ 本当に彼女って箱入り娘なんだね。「サラ金てなんなの？」なんて聞くんだもの。

Hontō ni kanojo tte hakoiri-musume nan da ne. "Sarakin tte nan na no?" nante kiku n' da mono.

She really is innocent of the ways of the world, isn't she? Hell, she asked me what a loan shark was.

Neko-kawaigari 猫可愛がり (Lit., "cat-loving") Endlessly spoiling a child [treating him or her like a pampered cat].

➡ 母は私の息子を猫可愛がりし、すっかり甘ったれにしてしまった。

Haha wa watashi no musuko o neko-kawaigari shi, sukkari amattare ni shite shimatta.

My mother has spoiled my kid rotten.

➡ おとうさん、そんなに道子のこと猫可愛がりしているとろくな娘にならないわよ。

Otōsan, sonna ni Michiko no koto neko-kawaigari shite iru to roku na musume ni naranai wa yo.

Woman: (to her husband) Dear, if you keep on spoiling Michiko like that, she'll never grow into a proper young lady.

Okini-iri お気に入り Pet; favorite.

➡ サチは先生のお気に入りだよね。

Sachi wa sensei no okini-iri da yo ne.

Sachi's the teacher's pet.

•• 子供の頃このクマのぬいぐるみがお気に入りだったのよ。

Kodomo no koro kono kuma no nuigurumi ga okini-iri datta no yo.

I loved this teddy bear when I was a kid.

Hiiki ひいき To side with; to prefer; to favor; to support. (⚡ This is used in two set constructions: *hiiki ni suru* (support; like; root for) and *hiiki suru* (favor; prefer [one over the other].)

•• ひいきにしているすもうとりが勝ってうれしかった。

Hiiki ni shite iru sumō-tori ga katte ureshikatta.

I was glad my favorite sumo wrestler won.

•• 私は子供の頃、兄ばかりが両親にひいきされていると思ってひがんでいた。

Watashi wa kodomo no koro, ani bakari ga ryōshin ni hiiki sarete iru to omotte higande ita.

When I was small I had a chip on my shoulder because I thought my parents always sided with my older brother.

Ekohiiki suru えこひいきする To be partial; to play favorites.

•• あの先生はいつでもえこひいきするのよ。

Ano sensei wa itsu demo ekohiiki suru no yo.

That teacher is always playing favorites.

•• 私は、それほど実力がないのに主役に選ばれたので、先生にえこひいきされていると陰口をたたかれた。

Watashi wa, sorehodo jitsuryoku ga nai no ni shuyaku ni erabareta no de, sensei ni ekohiiki sarete iru to kageguchi o tatakareta.

People were talking behind my back. They said the director was partial to me and chose me for the leading role in spite of my lack of talent.

Dekiai suru 溺愛する (Lit., "drowning love") To feel ex-

cessive affection; to love blindly; to dote on.

➡ 彼は、若くて美しい妻を溺愛した。

Kare wa, wakakute utsukushii tsuma o dekiai shita.

He was hopelessly in love with his young and beautiful wife.

➡ 彼女は一人息子を溺愛し、ガールフレンドにうっとうしがられている。

Kanojo wa hitori-musuko o dekiai shi, gārufurendo ni uttō-shigararete iru.

She so dotes on her only son that the boy's girlfriend can't stand her.

Mōai suru 盲愛する To feel a blind, reckless, all-consuming love (*not* of a sexual or romantic sort).

➡ 彼は盲愛していた孫娘が留学するのが寂しくてたまらない。

Kare wa mōai shite ita magomusume ga ryūgaku suru no ga sabishikute tamaranai.

He's devastated that his granddaughter, who means the world to him, is going overseas to study.

➡ A: 「うちの部長、お嬢さんを盲愛しているってうわさだよ」
　　B: 「そりゃそうだよ、あの年でやっとできた子なんだから」

　　A: Uchi no buchō, ojōsan o mōai shite iru tte uwasa da yo.
　　B: Sorya sō da yo, ano toshi de yatto dekita ko nan da kara.

A: Word has it that the department manager is completely nuts about his daughter.

B: Well, why wouldn't he be, at his age? She *is* his first child, after all.

Chōai 寵愛 (Lit., "patronage love") Attentions of; special attention from; favor with. (⚜ This term is now largely antiquated. It was used to refer to the protection or affection [often sexual] of a powerful figure such as a lord or governor.)

➡ 彼女は大富豪の寵愛を受けた。

Kanojo wa dai-fugō no chōai o uketa.

She received the attentions of a very wealthy man.

Hen'ai 偏愛 (Lit., "bias love") Partiality; favoritism.

➼ 彼女は、長男ばかりを偏愛した。

Kanojo wa, chōnan bakari o hen'ai shita.

She was always partial to her elder son.

TOUGH LOVE

Ai no muchi 愛の鞭 (Lit., "whip of love") Tough love; mistreating [someone], supposedly for his or her "own good."

➼ 彼は新入りをよく殴る。『愛の鞭だ』なんて言ってるけど、実際はただのしごきだ。

Kare wa shin'iri o yoku naguru. "Ai no muchi da" nante itte 'ru kedo, jissai wa tada no shigoki da.

He often hits the new members. He calls it "tough love," but it's really just plain old hazing.

➼ ボスが、あなたにきついこと言うのは愛の鞭なのよ。けっこうあなたのこと、買ってるみたいよ。

Bosu ga, anata ni kitsui koto iu no wa ai no muchi na no yo. Kekkō anata no koto, katte 'ru mitai yo.

When the boss says mean things to you, it's only because he cares. He actually thinks quite a lot of you.

Kokoro o oni ni suru 心を鬼にする (Lit., "make one's heart a demon") To take a hard-hearted attitude toward someone precisely because you care.

➼ わが子が寮から泣いて帰ってきても、母親は心を鬼にして追い返した。

Wagako ga ryō kara naite kaette kite mo, hahaoya wa kokoro o oni ni shite oikaeshita.

Even when our son came home from the dormitory crying, his mother just gritted her teeth and sent him back.

➼ A:「あんなに鬼のように怒らなくてもいいんじゃないかなあ」

B: 「ばかねえ、わが子を思えば母親は鬼になるものなのよ」

A: *Anna ni oni no yō ni okoranakute mo ii n' ja nai ka nā.*

B: *Baka nē, wagako o omoeba hahaoya wa oni ni naru mono na no yo.*

A: Do you really think it's necessary to fly into such a rage?

B: Don't be stupid. Any mother who cares about her kids has to be tough on them once in a while.

Kawaii ko ni wa tabi o sase yo 可愛い子には旅をさせよ (Lit., "Send a beloved child on a trip") To prepare a child for the future, it's best to send him or her out into the world.

➡ 母親: 「あの子はまだ十五ですよ、留学させるなんて早すぎます」

父親: 「本人がその気になっているんだし、いい機会だと思うよ。『可愛い子には旅をさせよ』というじゃないか」

Haha-oya: Ano ko wa mada jūgo desu yo, ryūgaku saseru nante hayasugi masu.

Chichi-oya: Honnin ga sono ki ni natte iru n' da shi, ii kikai da to omou yo. "Kawaii ko ni wa tabi o sase yo" to iu ja nai ka.

Mother: She's only fifteen—she's too young to study overseas.

Father: But she wants to go, and I think this is a good opportunity for her. You know the saying—"If you love your children, ship 'em off."

Kawaisa amatte nikusa hyaku-bai 可愛さあまって憎さ百倍 (Lit., "Too much affection, one hundred times the hatred") A love that is too intense turns quickly to hatred.

➡ A: 「彼女が婚約したとたん、部長は彼女に急に冷たくなったね」

B: 「自分に気があると思い込んでいたんでしょ。可愛さあまって憎さ百倍ってとこね」

A: *Kanojo ga kon'yaku shita totan, buchō wa kanojo ni kyū ni tsumetaku natta ne.*

B: *Jibun ni ki ga aru to omoikonde ita n' desho. Kawaisa amatte nikusa hyakubai tte toko ne.*

A: The minute she got engaged, the manager started treating her really coldly.

B: He probably thought she had a thing for *him*. Like they say—a whole lot of love turns into a whole lot of hate.

Mi o hiku 身をひく To voluntarily give up and withdraw from a situation or an endeavor [for someone else's sake]. (⚲ This phrase is used in a variety of situations, romantic and nonromantic alike.)

•• A: 「彼女、彼をあきらめたんだって?」
B: 「彼の出世と自分の年を考えて、身をひいたんだわ」

A: *Kanojo, kare o akirameta n' da tte?*
B: *Kare no shusse to jibun no toshi o kangaete, mi o hiita n' da wa.*

A: Is it true she gave up on their relationship?

B: She just thought it best to bow out, given the effect her age would have on his chances for promotion.

•• 彼は大きな失敗をして、あの仕事から身をひくことになったらしい。

Kare wa ōki na shippai o shite, ano shigoto kara mi o hiku koto ni natta rashii.

It seems he made some big mistake, and now he's taking himself off the project.

Miren ga aru 未練がある (Lit., "not yet soften") To not have gotten over; to feel continuing love for [someone] after an affair has ended; to carry a torch for.

•• 彼が結婚をしないのは、別れた恋人にまだ未練があるからだ。

Kare ga kekkon o shinai no wa, wakareta koibito ni mada miren ga aru kara da.

He hasn't married because he's still in love with the woman he broke up with.

•• マークったら、逃げた奥さんに未練たらたらなんだよ。

Māku ttara, nigeta okusan ni miren taratara nan da yo.

Poor Mark is still hopelessly in love with the wife who left him.

LOVE AND LIKING

Suki 好き   Like; be fond of; love. (⚡ Can be used in an extremely wide range of situations.)

•• ジャズ・ミュージックが好きなんだ。

Jazu myūzikku ga suki nan da.

I like jazz.

•• パパ、だあい好き！

Papa, dāisuki.

I love you, Papa!

•• あいつ、彼女を一目見て好きになってしまったらしいよ。

Aitsu, kanojo o hitome mite suki ni natte shimatta rashii yo.

He fell in love with her at first sight.

Kokoro o hikareru 心をひかれる   (Lit., "have one's heart pulled") To be attracted to; to be drawn to.

•• 私はスキーのコーチに初対面で心をひかれた。

Watashi wa sukii no kōchi ni shotai-men de kokoro o hikareta.

I was attracted to my ski coach the first time we met.

•• 彼女にはなぜか心ひかれるものがある。

Kanojo ni wa naze ka kokoro hikareru mono ga aru.

There's something attractive about her.

•• 毎朝駅で会う青年にひかれるようになった。

Mai-asa eki de au seinen ni hikareru yō ni natta.

I've gotten more and more attrancted to this boy I see every morning at the station.

Ki ga aru 気がある   (Lit., "have *ki*") To be interested in.

•• 「どうもあいつはお前に気があるみたいだな」

Dōmo aitsu wa omae ni ki ga aru mitai da na.

I think that person's interested in you.

➼ 「哲夫さんあなたに気があるのよ。あなたが独身かどうかさ
っき私に聞いてたもの」

*Tetsuo-san anata ni ki ga aru no yo. Anata ga dokushin ka
dō ka sakki watashi ni kiite 'ta mono.*

Know what? Tetsuo's interested in you. He asked me just
now if you were single.

Tokimeku/mune [kokoro] o tokimekasu ときめく/
胸(心)をときめかす (Lit., "palpitate/to make the heart
throb") To be thrilled; to be excited; to feel one's heart leap
with joy or anticipation.

➼ あしたはいよいよ彼に会えると思うと、胸がときめく。

Ashita wa iyoiyo kare ni aeru to omou to, mune ga tokimeku.

When I think about how I'll finally see him tomorrow, my
heart just leaps.

➼ 今日こそきっと彼にプロポーズされるだろうと、彼女は胸
をときめかした。

*Kyō koso kitto kare ni puropōzu sareru darō to, kanojo wa
mune o tokimekashita.*

Surely today would be the day he'd propose, she thought,
and her heart raced with excitement.

➼ もうすぐ春だと思うと、胸がときめく。

Mō sugu haru da to omou to, mune ga tokimeku.

It's exciting to think spring's almost here.

Dokidoki suru どきどきする To feel one's pulse race
with anxiety, fear, anticipation, etc.

➼ このホラー映画、筋は知っているのに、見るたびにどきど
きする。

*Kono horā eiga, suji wa shitte iru no ni, miru tabi ni doki-
doki suru.*

Even though I know the plot, this horror movie scares the
hell out of me every time I see it.

➼ あなたに初めてデートに誘われたとき、胸がどきどきしたわ。

Anata ni hajimete dēto ni sasowareta toki, mune ga doki-doki shita wa.

The first time you asked me out, my heart was just pounding.

Omou/omoi o yoseru 思う/思いを寄せる (Lit., "To think/to collect thoughts") To feel something for; to have [someone] on one's mind; to be hung up on; to have feelings for.

➼ ぼくが彼女を思う気持ちは本物だ。

Boku ga kanojo o omou kimochi wa honmono da.

My feelings for her are real.

➼ 君がどんなに彼女のことを思っても、彼女は別の男に夢中だから相手にしてくれないと思うよ。

Kimi ga donna ni kanojo no koto o omotte mo, kanojo wa betsu no otoko ni muchū da kara aite ni shite kurenai to omou yo.

I don't care how hung up on her you are. She's crazy about another guy, so I doubt if she'll give you the time of day.

➼ 彼女は上司にひそかに思いを寄せている。

Kanojo wa jōshi ni hisoka ni omoi o yosete iru.

She's secretly got a thing for the man she works under.

Akogareru あこがれる To be infatuated with; to be attracted to; to dream of; to aspire to.

➼ 昨日、ついにあこがれのパリに着きました。

Kinō, tsui ni akogare no Pari ni tsukimashita.

Yesterday I arrived in the city I've long dreamed of—Paris.

➼ 彼は弁護士にあこがれている。

Kare wa bengoshi ni akogarete iru.

His aspiration is to become a lawyer.

➼ 私は、彼女がひそかに彼にあこがれているのを知っている。

Watashi wa, kanojo ga hisoka ni kare ni akogarete iru no o shitte iru.

I know she's secretly in love with him.

➥ 彼女、勉強はトップだし、優しいし、美人だし、私たちの
あこがれの的なのよね。

*Kanojo, benkyō wa toppu da shi, yasashii shi, bijin da shi,
watashitachi no akogare no mato no yo ne.*

She's at the top of the class, and she's nice, and she's beautiful, so we all kind of wish we were her.

Shitau 慕う To long for; to idolize; to adore.

➥ 幼稚園の保母さんは、大勢の子供たちに慕われている。

*Yōchi-en no hobosan wa, ōzei no kodomo-tachi ni shita-
warete iru.*

Most of the kids in the kindergarten just idolize the teacher.

➥ 尚子、ずっと慕い続けてきた隣のお兄ちゃんとついにゴー
ルインしたんだって！

*Naoko, zutto shitaitsuzukete kita tonari no oniichan to tsui
ni gōru-in shita n' da tte!*

Naoko finally scored big-time with the neighbor she was
always mooning over—they're engaged to be married!
(⚓ *Gōru-in*, "to marry," originally comes from the Japanese
sporting term for "making a goal.")

Kataomoi 片思い (Lit., "one-way feelings") Unrequited love; one-sided love.

➥ 私、今好きな人がいるの。片思いだけど。

Watashi, ima suki na hito ga iru no. Kataomoi da kedo.

I'm in love with somebody now. It's unrequited, though.

➥ 磯のあわびの片思い

Iso no awabi no kataomoi

(Lit., "Unrequited love of abalone on the seashore") (⚓ A
metaphorical set phrase. Abalones are single-shelled mol-
lusks that cling to rocks along the coast in tidepools [and to
which the rocks don't cling back]).

Misomeru 見初める To feel, on first meeting, that some-

one is just the person you've been looking for.

•• 美人の姉は社長の御曹司に見初められ、玉の輿に乗った。

Bijin no ane wa shachō no on-zōshi ni misomerare, tama no koshi ni notta.

The president's son fell like a ton of bricks when he met my beautiful older sister, and now she's living like a queen.

•• 気難しい兄が見初めたのは、おおらかで明るい女性だった。

Kimuzukashii ani ga misometa no wa, ōraka de akarui josei datta.

The girl of my grumpy older brother's dreams turned out to be this very cheerful and easygoing person.

Horeru 惚れる To fall in love.

•• なんだ、お前彼女に惚れていたのか。実はおれもなんだ。

Nan da, omae kanojo ni horete ita no ka. Jitsu wa ore mo nan da.

So you're in love with her, are you. Well, actually, so am I.

•• 惚れてしまえば、あばたもえくぼ。

Horete shimaeba, abata mo ekubo.

(Lit., "When you fall in love with someone, their warts look like beauty marks.") Love is blind.

•• オードリーはとっても惚れっぽい。

Ōdorii wa tottemo horeppoi.

Audrey falls in love at the drop of a hat.

Hitome-bore 一目惚れ Love at first sight.

•• お隣の奥さん、ご主人に一目惚れだったんですって。

Otonari no okusan, go-shujin ni hitome-bore datta n' desu tte.

The lady next door says she fell in love with her husband at first sight.

•• この茶碗、骨董品屋で見かけて、一目惚れしちゃってねえ、とうとう買ってしまったんだ。

Kono chawan, kottōhin-ya de mikakete, hitome-bore shichatte nē, tōtō katte shimatta n' da.

When I found this teacup in the antique shop, I fell in love with it right away and just had to buy it.

Koi 恋 Love (with at least a slight sexual nuance).

➻ 恋をすると、四六時中相手のことばかり考えて、仕事も手につかない。

Koi o suru to, shirokuji-chū aite no koto bakari kangaete, shigoto mo te ni tsukanai.

When I'm in love with someone, that person's always on my mind and I can't get any work done.

➻ 一度でいいから、めくるめくような恋がしたい。

Ichido de ii kara, mekurumeku yō na koi ga shitai.

Just once I'd like to have a really passionate love affair.

➻ 彼女はまだ恋に恋する年頃だ。

Kanojo wa mada koi ni koi suru toshigoro da.

She's still at the age where she's in love with love.

➻ 恋は盲目。

Koi wa mōmoku.

"Love is blind.

Koigokoro 恋心 (Lit., "love heart") Feelings of love.

➻ 彼は入院中、親切に世話をしてくれた若い看護婦に淡い恋心を抱いた。

Kare wa nyūin-chū, shinsetsu ni sewa o shite kureta wakai kango-fu ni awai koigokoro o idaita.

When he was in the hospital, he came down with a mild case of love for the young nurse who took such good care of him.

Koi no yokan 恋の予感 (Lit., "premonition of love") A sense, on first meeting, that something is going to evolve into love.

➻ 彼女を紹介されたとき、僕には恋の予感があった。

Kanojo o shōkai sareta toki, boku ni wa koi no yokan ga atta.

The moment we were introduced, I had a hunch we might fall in love.

Hatsukoi 初恋 First love; puppy love.

➡ 私の初恋は中学一年のときで、相手はテニス部のキャプテンだった。

Watashi no hatsukoi wa chūgaku ichinen no toki de, aite wa tenisu-bu no kyaputen datta.

I first fell in love when I was in sixth grade, with the captain of the tennis team.

➡ 彼女は初恋の相手と結ばれた。

Kanojo wa hatsukoi no aite to musubareta.

She married her first love.

Koi ni ochiru 恋に落ちる To fall in love.

➡ 二人は旅先のベニスで知り合い、やがて恋に落ちた。

Futari wa tabisaki no Benisu de shiriai, yagate koi ni ochita.

They met in Venice while traveling and eventually fell in love.

➡ 私たち『恋に落ちて』っていう映画を見に行って、恋に落ちちゃった！

Watashitachi "Koi ni ochite" tte iu eiga o mi ni itte, koi ni ochichatta!

We went to see a movie called "Falling in Love," and damned if we didn't fall in love.

Koi kogareru 恋焦がれる (Lit., "burning love") To go crazy [with love] over; to like [someone] so much it drives you nuts.

➡ マリアはトニーに恋焦がれている。

Maria wa Tonii ni koi kogarete iru.

Maria's going out of her head over Tony.

Ren'ai 恋愛 Romantic and sexual love; a love affair.

➡ 二人の交際は長いけれど、いわゆる恋愛には発展しなかった。

Futari no kōsai wa nagai keredo, iwayuru ren'ai ni wa hatten shinakatta.

They've known each other a long time, but it's never developed into what you could call a love affair.

➡ 彼女に対して次第に恋愛感情がわいてきた。

Kanojo ni taishite shidai ni ren'ai kanjō ga waite kita.

I gradually began to have feelings of love for her.

Koibito 恋人 A lover; lovers.

➡ このごろとてもきれいになったね。恋人でもできたんじゃないの？

Konogoro totemo kirei ni natta ne. Koibito de mo dekita n' ja nai no?

You're more beautiful than ever these days. Did you find yourself a lover or something?

➡ 彼は、「友達以上、恋人未満」ね。

Kare wa "tomodachi ijō, koibito miman" ne.

He's more than a friend, but not quite a lover.

Ryō-omoi 両思い Equal fondness [for each other]; love that is reciprocated.

➡ あの二人、てっきり彼女の片思いだと思っていたけど、意外にも両思いだった。

Ano futari, tekkiri kanojo no kataomoi da to omotte ita kedo, igai ni mo ryō-omoi datta.

I thought her love for him was unrequited and then, surprisingly enough, it turned out to be mutual.

➡ 彼女と両思いになれますように！

Kanojo to ryō-omoi ni naremaru yō ni!

Just let her feel the same way too!

Ayashii/kusai 怪しい/くさい Suspicious/smelly (terms used to tease or gossip about a pair who seem to be just a

bit more intimate than other people, implying that they've secretly got something going).

➻ あの二人なんとなく怪しいね、できてるんじゃないの？

Ano futari nanto naku ayashii ne, dekite 'ru n' ja nai no?

There's something suspicious about those two. You think they've got something going on?

➻ A: 「リサとデイブが、仲良くコンビニから出てくるのを見ちゃった！」

B: 「なんだかくさいね」

A: Lisa to Deibu ga, naka-yoku konbini kara dete kuru no o michatta!

B: Nan da ka kusai ne.

A: I saw Lisa and Dave coming out of a convenience store together, and they were looking awfully chummy!

B: Something fishy going on there.

Oyasukunai お安くない (Lit., "not cheap") Another way of teasing or gossiping about someone one suspects of romantic involvement.

➻ 彼女がおべんとうを作ってくれたって？　お安くないね。

Kanojo ga obentō o tsukutte kureta tte? Oyasukunai ne.

She made you a box lunch? Must be love.

➻ A: 「君にしては、派手なセーター着てるじゃない？」

B: 「なんだか知らないけれど、隣のクラスの陽子が編んでくれたんだ」

A: 「ふうん、お安くないんじゃない？」

A: Kimi ni shite wa, hade na sētā kite 'ru ja nai?

B: Nan da ka shiranai kedo, tonari no kurasu no Yōko ga ande kureta n' da.

A: Fūn, oyasukunai n' ja nai?

A: Some sweater! Pretty flashy for you, isn't it?

B: Don't ask me why, but that girl Yoko in the next class made it for me.

A: Duh! Sounds like love to me.

Oiraku no koi 老いらくの恋 (Lit., "senior love") A love

that comes along when one is old.

↝ おばあちゃんはこのごろおしゃれになったね。老いらくの
恋でもしているのかな？

Obāchan wa konogoro oshare ni natta ne. Oiraku no koi de mo shite iru no ka na?

Grandma's sure been stylin' lately. You think she's in love?

↝ A: 「おじいちゃんに恋人ができたんだって？　老いらくの
　　　恋だな」
　　B: 「ご本人は初恋だ、とか言っているよ」

A: Ojiichan ni koibito ga dekita n' da tte? Oiraku no koi da na.
B: Go-honnin wa hatsukoi da, to ka itte iru yo.

A: Granddad's got a girlfriend? There's life in the old dog yet, eh?
B: That isn't how he'd put it—he calls it "puppy love."

Ai suru 愛する To love.

↝ 人を愛することはすばらしいことだ。

Hito o ai suru koto wa subarashii koto da.

It's a wonderful thing to love someone.

↝ 少女は気だてが良くてだれからも愛されていた。

Shōjo wa kidate ga yokute dare kara mo ai sarete ita.

The little girl was so good-natured that everyone loved her.

↝ 女：「ねえ、私のこと愛してる？」
　　男：「もちろん愛してるに決まってるだろ」
　　女：「じゃあ、証明してよ！」

Onna: Nē, watashi no koto ai shite 'ru?
Otoko: Mochiron ai shite 'ru ni kimatte 'ru daro.
Onna: Jā, shōmei shite yo!

Woman: Do you love me?
Man:　　Of course I love you. What do you think?
Woman: So show me!

Aijō 愛情 (Lit., "love feeling") Love; warmth; affection.

➾ 彼女は子供たちに深い愛情を注いだ。

Kanojo wa kodomo-tachi ni fukai aijō o sosoida.

She gave her children lots of love.

➾ A:「あの子、いじめっ子で先生たちずいぶん手を焼いてる
　　らしいわよ」

　B:「親が放ったらかしだから、愛情に飢えてるんじゃない
　　の？」

　A: Ano ko, ijimekko de sensei-tachi zuibun te o yaite 'ru
　　rashii wa yo.

　B: Oya ga hottarakashi da kara, aijō ni uete 'ru n' ja nai
　　no?

　A: That kid's a real little bully. She's caused the teachers
　　all sorts of problems.

　B: Her parents completely neglected her, so she's probably
　　starved for affection.

Ai wa oshimi naku ataeru 愛は惜しみなく与える To
love without restraint or bounds; to give everything for love.

➾ A:「彼女、男に貢ぐために横領したんだって」

　B:「『愛は惜しみなく与える』っていうのを、間違って理
　　解しちゃったわけだね」

　A: Kanojo, otoko ni mitsugu tame ni ōryō shitan datte.

　B: "Ai wa oshimi naku ataeru" tte iu no o, machigatte rikai
　　shichatta wake da ne.

　A: I hear she embezzled money in order to give it to some
　　guy.

　B: Seems like she went a little overboard with the concept
　　of giving everything for love.

Jun'ai 純愛 True love; pure, romantic love.

➾ 純愛なんて今時はやらないかもしれないけど、一途に人を
愛するというのはすばらしいんじゃない？

Jun'ai nante imadoki hayaranai ka mo shirenai kedo,
ichizu ni hito o aisuru to iu no wa subarashii n' ja nai?

I'm not sure people go in for true love much any more. But
it must be wonderful to love one person with all your heart.

Ai ga areba toshi no sa nante 愛があれば年の差なんて ("If there's love, what's a little age difference?") (❀ Often used to play down an age difference that one actually considers embarrassing.)

❧ 親子ほど年が離れていても、愛があれば年の差なんて関係ない。

Oyako hodo toshi ga hanarete ite mo, ai ga areba toshi no sa nante kankei nai.

So what if I'm old enough to be her father? If two people love each other, what difference does age make?

❧ A: 「『愛があれば年の差なんて』とはいうものの、二十歳年下の彼じゃあちょっと頼りないよね」

B: 「当たり前よ、二十歳下っていったらまだ五歳じゃないの！」

A: "Ai ga areba toshi no sa nante" to wa iu mono no, niju-ssai toshishita no kare jā chotto tayorinai yo ne.

B: Atarimae yo, niju-ssai toshi shita tte ittara mada gosai ja nai no?

A: They say age is irrelevant when it comes to love, but I'd find a guy twenty years younger than me a little hard to depend on, wouldn't you?

B: Well, yeah! But in my case, that would make him five years old.

Sōshi-sōai 相思相愛 (Lit., "think together, love together") To love and be loved back; to be in love [with one another].

❧ おじいちゃんとおばあちゃんは相思相愛で、困難を乗り越えて一緒になったんだよ。

Ojiichan to obāchan wa sōshi-sōai de, konnan o norikoete issho ni nattan da yo.

Grandpa and Grandma were deeply in love, and overcame all sorts of obstacles to be together.

❧ 彼らは人もうらやむほどの相思相愛の仲だ。

Karera wa hito mo urayamu hodo no sōshi-sōai no naka da.

They're so in love that people envy them.

Kon'yaku suru 婚約する To become engaged [to be married].

⊸ 2年の交際の後、私たちは婚約した。

Ninen no kōsai no ato, watashitachi wa kon'yaku shita.

We became engaged after a two-year courtship.

⊸ 彼の浮気で、婚約は解消になった。

Kare no uwaki de, kon'yaku wa kaishō ni natta.

The engagement was broken off because he was fooling around.

Tenabe sagete mo 手鍋下げても (Lit., "Even with pan in hand") Willingness to live even in poverty, provided it's with the man one loves.

⊸ 手鍋下げてもあなたについて行くわ。

Tenabe sagete mo anata ni tsuite iku wa.

Who cares about money? I just want to be with you.

Kekkon suru 結婚する To marry; to wed.

⊸ まさかあなたが彼と結婚するとは思いませんでした。

Masaka anata ga kare to kekkon suru to wa omoimasen deshita.

I never thought you'd marry him.

⊸ 結婚なんて、忍耐以外のなにものでもないよ。

Kekkon nante, nintai igai no nanimono de mo nai yo.

Marriage is nothing but perseverance.

Aisai-ka 愛妻家 (Lit., "lover of a wife") A husband who really loves his wife.

⊸ A: 「彼は、自他ともに認める愛妻家だ」
B: 「そうかなあ、恐妻家じゃないの？」

A: Kare wa, jita tomo ni mitomeru aisai-ka da.
B: Sō ka nā, kyōsai-ka ja nai no?

A: There's no denying he's a devoted husband.
B: Hm. Devoted, or just henpecked?

Koi-nyōbō 恋女房 (Lit., "beloved wife") A woman one married for love, and whom one still loves dearly.

➡ 僕は恋女房を裏切るようなことはしない。

Boku wa koi-nyōbō o uragiru yō na koto wa shinai.

I'd never do anything to betray my beloved wife.

COMING ON STRONG

Kudoku 口説く To come on to; to hit on; to sweet-talk.

➡ 良樹ったら、女性と見るとすぐ口説こうとするんだから……。

Yoshiki ttara, josei to miru to sugu kudokō to suru n' da kara ...

Yoshiki no sooner sees a woman than he tries to hit on her.

➡ 彼女を口説いたってむだだよ。男には興味ないんだから。

Kanojo o kudoita tte muda da yo. Otoko ni wa kyōmi nai n' da kara.

No use trying to sweet-talk her. She's not interested in men.

Iiyoru 言い寄る To come on to; to try to seduce; to make a pass at; to put the make on.

➡ 由香子は美人なので、言い寄る男も少なくない。

Yukako wa bijin nanode, iiyoru otoko mo sukunakunai.

Yukako's a knockout, so lots of men come on to her.

➡ A: 「私、どんなにすてきな男性が言い寄ってきても相手に
　　　しないわ」
　 B: 「まあ、そんな心配もないと思うけど……」

　A: Watashi, donna ni suteki na dansei ga iiyotte kite mo aite ni shinai wa.

　B: Mā, sonna shinpai mo nai to omou kedo ...

　A: I wouldn't let even the sexiest man seduce me.

　B: Well, I wouldn't worry about that if I were you.

Yūwaku suru 誘惑する To seduce.

➼ ルーシーは若い男を誘惑した。

Lūcii wa wakai otoko o yūwaku shita.

Lucy seduced some young guy.

➼ あんな男の誘惑になんか乗ってはいけないよ。プレイボーイで有名なんだから……。

Anna otoko no yūwaku ni nanka notte wa ikenai yo. Purei-bōi de yūmei nan da kara …

Don't go letting that guy seduce you. Everybody knows what a playboy he is.

Teren-tekuda 手練手管 Every trick in the book; [feminine] wiles; technique

➼ A: 「彼女、ついに英雄と婚約したんだって」
B: 「へえ、それこそ手練手管でだましたんだろうね」

A: Kanojo, tsui ni Hideo to kon'yaku shita n' datte.
B: Hē, sore koso teren-tekuda de tamashita n' darō ne.

A: I hear she and Hideo ended up getting engaged.
B: Yeah? She must've used every trick in the book to snag him.

Oshi no itte 押しの一手 (Lit., "pushing, and pushing alone") To pursue [someone] aggressively; to not take no for an answer.

➼ ボブは陽子の押しの一手についその気にさせられた。

Bobu wa Yōko no oshi no itte ni tsui sono ki ni saserareta.

Yoko kept hammering on Bob till he finally got with the program.

➼ A: 「ねえ、どうやってあんなかわいい子を彼女にできたの？」
B: 「そりゃもう、『押しの一手』だけ」

A: Nē, dō yatte anna kawaii ko o kanojo ni dekita no?
B: Sorya mō, "oshi no itte" dake.

A: How did you get such a cute girlfriend?
B: Simple—I just wouldn't take no for an answer.

Irome o tsukau 色目を使う (Lit., "use erotic [colored]

eyes") To make eyes at; to give [someone] the eye; to look at [someone] with bedroom eyes. (⚥ Primarily a feminine technique.)

➻ さつきはだれでも若い男を見ると色目を使う。

Satsuki wa dare de mo wakai otoko o miru to irome o tsukau.

Satsuki gives the eye to every young man she sees.

➻ ちょっと、私の彼に色目を使わないでよ！

Chotto, watashi no kare ni irome o tsukawanaide yo!"

Hey! Don't you be giving my boyfriend that look!

➻ 会長の息子に色目を使っても無駄だよ。きれいな婚約者がいるんだから。

Kaichō no musuko ni irome o tsukatte mo muda da yo. Kirei na kon'yaku-sha ga iru n' da kara.

No use using those bedroom eyes on the chairman's son. He's got a beautiful fiancée.

WALKING ON AIR

Zokkon ぞっこん (Lit., "from the bottom root") Head over heels in love with; crazy about.

➻ 僕は、彼女にぞっこんまいっている。

Boku wa, kanojo ni zokkon maitte iru.

He's head over heels in love with her.

➻ 妹のやつ、お前にぞっこんなんだ、つき合ってやってくれないか。

Imōto no yatsu, omae ni zokkon nan da, tsukiatte yatte kurenai ka.

My little sister's crazy about you. Would you mind asking her out?

Muchū 夢中 (Lit., "in the midst of a dream") Only having eyes for; really into; fascinated by; absorbed in.

➻ 兄は新しい恋人に夢中になったが、じきにふられてしまった。

Ani wa atarashii koibito ni muchū ni natta ga, jiki ni fu-rarete shimatta.

My brother was ecstatic about his new girlfriend, but she dumped him soon enough.

➥ 息子はアイドル歌手に夢中だ。

Musuko wa aidoru kashu ni muchū da.

Our son is obsessed with some pop singer.

➥ 今、私は古典文学に夢中になっている。

Ima, watashi wa koten-bungaku ni muchū ni natte iru.

I'm totally into classical Japanese literature right now.

Kubittake 首ったけ (Lit., "up to one's neck") Head over heels for; crazy about.

➥ 彼は僕の妹に首ったけで、暇さえあればデートに誘い出す。

Kare wa boku no imōto ni kubittake de, hima sae areba dēto ni sasoidasu.

He's nuts about my sister. Whenever he gets a little time free, he asks her out.

➥ うちのお父さん、今でもお母さんに首ったけなんだよ。

Uchi no otōsan, ima de mo okāsan ni kubittake nan da yo.

Our father's still madly in love with our mother.

Mairu まいる To be gone on; to be taken with. (⚓ This word is used in the "-*tte*" form: *maitte iru, maitte ita, maitte shimatta*, etc.

➥ 僕は彼女にすっかりまいっている。

Boku wa kanojo ni sukkari maitte iru.

I've completely lost my head over her.

➥ 彼はさゆりの誘惑に、ころりとまいってしまった。

Kare wa Sayuri no yūwaku ni, korori to maitte shimatta.

He didn't put up much of a fight when Sayuri seduced him.

Nomerikomu のめり込む (Lit., "stumble into") To get in too deep; to become obsessed; to get hooked.

➸ あの女とはちょっと遊びのつもりだったのに、すっかりのめり込んでしまった。

Ano onna to wa chotto asobi no tsumori datta no ni, sukkari nomerikonde shimatta.

I was just out for a good time at first, but ended up totally involved with her.

➸ 誠は、競馬にのめり込んで会社を辞めた。

Makoto wa, keiba ni nomerikonde kaisha o yameta.

Makoto became so obsessed with the horses he quit his job.

Kokoro o ubawareru 心を奪われる To lose one's heart to.

➸ 十代の頃、「スティング」を見てロバート・レッドフォードにすっかり心を奪われちゃったのよね。

Jūdai no koro, "Sutingu" o mite Robāto Reddofōdo ni sukkari kokoro o ubawarechatta no yo ne.

When I was in my teens I saw "The Sting" and lost my heart to Robert Redford.

➸ 彼女は女たらしの次郎にすっかり心を奪われてしまった。

Kanojo wa onna-tarashi no Jirō ni sukkari kokoro o ubawarete shimatta.

That womanizer Jirō stole her heart.

Netsu o ageru/onetsu 熱を上げる/お熱 (Lit., "raise the heat/become feverish") To have the hots for; to be hot for; to be keen on.

➸ 妹はあの歌手に熱を上げている。

Imōto wa ano kashu ni netsu o agete iru.

My little sister has the hots for that singer.

➸ クレアはアダムにお熱だ。

Kurea wa Adamu ni onetsu da.

Crea is pretty keen on Adam.

Noboseru のぼせる (Lit., "have the blood rush to one's

head") To be bonkers about; to be infatuated with.

⇔ 彼は新任の婦人警官にのぼせている。

Kare wa shinnin no fujin-keikan ni nobosete iru.

He's lost his head over the new policewoman.

⇔ あれほどの美人なら、正輝がのぼせるのも無理はない。

Are hodo no bijin nara, Masaki ga noboseru no mo muri wa nai.

A woman that beautiful—no wonder Masaki flipped for her.

Pōtto naru ポーッとなる To space out [in the presence of someone one likes]; to have one's head in the clouds.

⇔ 彼にじっと見つめられ、ポーッとなってしまった。

Kare ni jiitto mitsumerare, pōtto natte shimatta.

He kept staring at me, and I just completely spaced out.

⇔ 妹は、あこがれの先輩に声をかけられポーッとしている。

Imōto wa, akogare no senpai ni koe o kakerare pōtto shite iru.

The upperclassman my sister has a crush on spoke to her, and now she's walking on air.

Uttori suru うっとりする To feel as if one is in a dream.

⇔ 由美は恋人のことを考えてうっとりした目をした。

Yumi wa koibito no koto o kangaete uttori shita me o shita.

Thinking about her lover, Yumi got a dreamy look in her eyes.

Go-shūshin ご執心 (Lit., "honorable devotion") Devoted to; thoroughly taken with; hung up on. (⚹ The "*go*" prefix, usually respectful, is here used in a playful and sarcastic way.)

⇔ ねえ、ずいぶんリンダにご執心のようだね。

Nē, zuibun Rinda ni go-shūshin no yō da ne.

You're pretty devoted to Linda, aren't you.

⇔ 社長は秘書にご執心だ。

Shachō wa hisho ni go-shūshin da.

The boss is absolutely hung up on his secretary.

Oboreru 溺れる (Lit., "drown") To be so obsessed as to lose all reason; to go way overboard.

➺ まじめだった男が妻に逃げられたとたんに酒色に溺れるようになってしまった。

Majime datta otoko ga tsuma ni nigerareta totan ni shu-shoku ni oboreru yō ni natte shimatta.

He had been a serious man, but no sooner had his wife left him than he threw himself into drinking and womanizing.

➺ 太郎はすっかり花子に溺れている。

Tarō wa sukkari Hanako ni oborete iru.

Taro is completely hooked on Hanako.

Atsui shisen 熱い視線 (Lit., "hot gaze") A passionate stare; a burning gaze.

➺ 背後に熱い視線を感じて振り向くと、そこに彼女が立っていた。

Haigo ni atsui shisen o kanjite furimuku to, soko ni kanojo ga tatte ita.

I felt someone's eyes burning into me, and when I turned around, there she stood.

➺ 浩子はバスケット部の先輩に熱い視線を送っている。

Hiroko wa basuketto-bu no senpai ni atsui shisen o okutte iru.

Hiroko is giving the most intense looks to one of the older guys on the basketball team.

Amai kotoba 甘い言葉 (Lit., "sweet words") Sweet talk; cajolery; flattery.

➺ エリザベスは好きな男に甘い言葉をささやかれ、有頂天になってしまった。

Elizabesu wa suki na otoko ni amai kotoba o sasayakare, uchō-ten ni natte shimatta.

When the guy she liked murmured sweet nothings in her ear, Elizabeth nearly lost it.

➾ ガイにはきっと下心があるんだから、甘い言葉に騙されてはいけないよ。

Gai ni wa kitto shitagokoro ga aru n' da kara, amai kotoba ni damasarete wa ikenai yo.

Guy's always got some ulterior motive, so he'll say all sorts of sweet things, but don't believe a word of it.

Naka-mutsumajii 仲むつまじい Intimate; mutually caring; harmonious.

➾ 夫婦が健康で仲むつまじく暮らせれば、財産なんかなくても幸せだ。

Fūfu ga kenkō de naka-mutsumajiku kuraseba, zaisan nanka nakute mo shiawase da.

As long as a husband and wife are healthy and care for each other, they don't need a fortune to be happy.

➾ 公園を毎日一緒に散歩する、仲むつまじい老夫婦がいる。

Kōen o mainichi issho ni sanpo suru, naka-mutsumajii rōfūfu ga iru.

There is an elderly couple who get along so well that they even go for walks in the park together every day.

Daisuki 大好き Like very much; love.

➾ 僕は彼女のさりげない優しさが大好きだ。

Boku wa kanojo no sarigenai yasashisa ga daisuki da.

She has a natural kindness that I just love.

➾ 父は釣りが大好きです。

Chichi wa tsuri ga daisuki desu.

Dad loves fishing.

➾ 彼が大好き。

Kare ga daisuki.

I really, really like him.

Suki de suki de tamaranai 好きで好きでたまらない

Liking someone or something so much that one can hardly bear it.

➻ ほら、「まいを好きで好きでたまらない」って、顔に書いてあるよ！

Hora, "Mai o suki de suki de tamaranai" tte, kao ni kaite aru yo!

Look at you. You're so crazy about Mai you can hardly stand it. It's written all over your face!

➻ 彼は私なんか眼中にないのに、私は彼が好きで好きでたまらない。

Kare wa watashi nanka ganchū ni nai no ni, watashi wa kare ga suki de suki de tamaranai.

I like him so much it's driving me mad, and he doesn't even know I exist.

Sai-ai 最愛 Dearest; beloved.

➻ 彼は私の最愛の人です。

Kare wa watashi no sai-ai no hito desu.

I love him immensely.

➻ 彼女は去年、最愛の息子をなくした。

Kanojo wa kyonen, sai-ai no musuko o nakushita.

She lost her dear son last year.

Netsu-ai suru 熱愛する To love passionately.

➻ あの二人は熱愛中だ。

Ano futari wa netsuai-chū da.

Those two are madly in love.

➻ あの女優は、年下のプロレスラーと熱愛宣言をして週刊誌で騒がれた。

Ano joyū wa, toshishita no puro-resurā to netsu-ai sengen o shite shū-kanshi de sawagareta.

She's the actress the weeklies made such a fuss over when

she announced her burning love for a younger pro wrestler.

➡ 彼は、その才能にあふれた若い弟子を熱愛している。

Kare wa, sono sainō ni afureta wakai deshi o netsu-ai shite iru.

He's passionately in love with that talented young pupil of his.

LOVING TO EXCESS

Betabore べた惚れ Loving to distraction; drunk with love.

➡ 彼ったら私にべた惚れなの。

Kare ttara watashi ni betabore na no.

He's absolutely mad about me.

Meromero めろめろ A sucker for; a pushover; a softie.

➡ 子供には厳しかった父だが、孫にはめろめろだ。

Kodomo ni wa kibishikatta chichi da ga, mago ni wa meromero da.

Dad was strict with his own kids, but he's a pushover for his grandchildren.

➡ 彼は若い妻にめろめろで、なんでも言うことを聞いてしまう。

Kare wa wakai tsuma ni meromero de, nandemo iu koto o kiite shimau.

He's a sucker for his young bride. He'll do anything she says.

Mejiri o sageru 目尻を下げる (Lit., "lower the outer corners of the eyes") To wear a contented, happy expression; to glow with contentment; to beam with pleasure.

➡ 君、彼女の話になると目尻が下がりっぱなしだよ。

Kimi, kanojo no hanashi ni naru to mejiri ga sagarippanashi da yo.

Man, whenever you talk about her you get this silly grin on your face.

Atsuatsu あつあつ Hotsy-totsy; hot and heavy; unable to keep their hands off (one another).

➼ あの二人は、結婚したばかりであつあつだ。

Ano futari wa, kekkon shita bakari de atsuatsu da.

Those two just got married and can't keep their hands off each other.

➼ あつあつなのも時間の問題さ。

Atsuatsu na no mo jikan no mondai sa.

If it's just a sexual thing, it won't last.

Ichaicha suru/ichatsuku いちゃいちゃする/いちゃつく To make out; to pet; to neck.

➼ あの二人ときたら人前でも平気でいちゃいちゃするんだから、まったく見ちゃいられない。

Ano futari to kitara hitomae de mo heiki de ichaicha suru n' dakara, mattaku micha irarenai.

Those two don't think anything of making out right in front of people. Who the hell wants to see that?

➼ 電車の中でいちゃついているカップルを見ると、こっちが恥ずかしくなる。

Densha no naka de icha-tsuite iru kappuru o miru to, kotchi ga hazukashiku naru.

It's embarrassing when you see a couple on the train who are all over each other.

Betabeta suru べたべたする To be all over someone; to hang all over someone; to be clingy or needy.

➼ いくら好きな男でも、四六時中べたべたされたんじゃうんざりする。

Ikura suki na otoko de mo, shirokuji-chū betabeta sareta n' ja unzari suru.

I don't care how much I like someone, if he's constantly hanging onto me like that it makes me sick.

➼ 夫:「親の前で、べたべたするなよ」

妻：「あら、お父さんたちを安心させようと思っただけよ。
　　本当の私たち見たら、悲しむでしょ？」

Otto: *Oya no mae de, betabeta suru na yo.*

Tsuma: *Ara, otōsan-tachi o anshin saseyō to omotta dake*
          yo. Hontō no watashitachi mitara, kanashimu
          desho?

Husband: Quit being so lovey-dovey in front of my parents.

Wife: Well! I was just trying to set their minds at ease.
         Don't you think it would make them sad to see
         how we really are?

Deredere suru でれでれする To fawn over (someone).

●➡ あいつは彼女にぞっこんで、もうでれでれしっぱなしだ。

Aitsu wa kanojo ni zokkon de, mō deredere shippanashi da.

He's nuts about her. Fawns over her constantly.

Hana no shita o nobasu/hana no shita o nagaku suru 鼻の下を伸ばす/鼻の下を長くする (Lit., "make the space below one's nose long") To leer at; to drool over; to have a lecherous look on one's face.

●➡ 女と見るとすぐ鼻の下を長くして、しょうがない奴だ。

Onna to miru to sugu hana no shita o nagaku shite, shō ga nai yatsu da.

Can't take you anywhere, can we? You see a woman and start drooling like a dog.

●➡ パパ！新体操を見て、鼻の下のばさないで！

Papa! Shin-taisō o mite, hana no shita nobasanaide!

Papa! This is rhythmic gymnastics, not a girlie show. Wipe that lecherous look off your face!

Koi ni mi o yatsusu 恋に身をやつす To waste away with love; to grow visibly thinner from worrying over one's love life

●➡ 兄は仕事もそっちのけで、恋に身をやつしている。

Ani wa shigoto mo sotchinoke de, koi ni mi o yatsushite iru.

My brother's neglecting his work and losing weight, all because of his girlfriend.

Koi wa mōmoku 恋は盲目 "Love is blind"

••『桃子の新しい彼見た？ いったいどこがいいのかしら。『恋は盲目』というけど、ほんとね」

Momoko no atarashii kare mita? Ittai doko ga ii no kashira.
"Koi wa mōmoku" to iu kedo, honto ne.

Did you see Momoko's new boyfriend? What on earth does she see in him? I guess it's true what they say—"Love is blind."

Koi ni jōge no sabetsu nashi/koi ni jōge no hedate nashi 恋に上下の差別なし/恋に上下の隔てなし

("Love knows no distinction [barrier] between high and low.") "Love doesn't discriminate on the basis of social status or wealth."

••「恋に上下の差別なし」といってね、貧乏でも金持ちでも恋する気持ちは同じはずだ。

"Koi ni jōge no sabetsu nashi" to itte ne, binbō de mo kane-mochi de mo koi suru kimochi wa onaji hazu da.

They say love doesn't discriminate—you can fall in love with a rich man just as easily as with a poor one.

Tereru 照れる To feel slightly embarrassed or awkward.

••そんなに誉められると照れるなあ。

Sonna ni homerareru to tereru nā.

I feel awkward when someone praises me so much.

••あんなに見せつけられるとこっちのほうが照れちゃうよ。

Anna ni misetsukerareru to kotchi no hō ga terechau yo.

It's embarrassing when people go at it right in front of you like that.

Norokeru のろける To boast in an annoying way about one's great relationship with a spouse or lover.

••雅子ってば「うちの主人、とっても優しくて頼りになるの

よ」なんてのろけるんだもの聞いちゃいられない。

Masako tteba "Uchi no shujin, tottemo yasashikute tayori ni naru no yo" nante norokeru n' da mono kiicha irarenai.

That Masako! I can't listen to any more of her "My husband's so sweet, my husband's so reliable" crap.

- A: 「彼、私の手料理が食べたいといって、どんなに遅くなっても、うちで食事するのよ、困っちゃう」
- B: 「あら、それって、おのろけでしょ」

A: Kare, watashi no te-ryōri ga tabetai to itte, donna ni osoku natte mo, uchi de shokuji suru no yo, komatchau.
B: Ara, sore tte, onoroke desho.

A: We always eat at home, no matter how late he gets back, because he says he likes my cooking. It's a real problem!
B: Hey, this is supposed to be a complaint, right?

Gochisōsama ごちそうさま ("Thanks for the treat") A set phrase used sarcastically in reply to someone's boast about a close relationship with a lover.

- A: 「彼ったら、私のこと世界で一番好きだって」
- B: 「あっそう、ごちそうさま」

A: Kare ttara, watashi no koto sekai de ichiban suki da tte.
B: A sō, gochisōsama.

A: He's so silly. He said he loves me more than anyone else in the whole world.
B: Oh, really? Well, thanks ever so much for sharing.

Aterareru あてられる (Lit., "be exposed") To be stuck in the company of a pair of passionate lovers.

- 新婚家庭に遊びにいったら、すっかりあてられてまいったよ。

Shinkon katei ni asobi ni ittara, sukkari aterarete maitta yo.

When I went over to the newlyweds' house, I was exposed to some pretty embarrassing little love scenes.

Tade kū mushi mo sukizuki 蓼食う虫も好きずき (Lit., "some bugs prefer nettles") "It takes all kinds (to make a world)"; "to each his own"; "there's no accounting for taste."

●➞ あんなイヤミな女はいないと思うけれど、蓼食う虫も好きずきで、彼女とつき合いたいという男がいる。

Anna iyami na onna wa inai to omou kedo, tade kū mushi mo sukizuki de, kanojo to tsukiaitai to iu otoko ga iru.

I think she's an awful woman, but I know this guy who wants to go out with her. To each his own, I guess.

Teishu no suki na aka ebōshi 亭主の好きな赤烏帽子

(Lit., "a husband's beloved red lacquer hat") "The husband's taste is also his wife's." (A saying used to refer to a wife's willingness to go along with her husband's eccentric tastes.)

●➞ A:「うちのパパ、お刺身にイチゴジャムつけて食べるの好きなのよ」

B:「いくら『亭主の好きな赤烏帽子』でも、あなたまですることないじゃないの！」

A: Uchi no papa, osashimi ni ichigo jamu tsukete taberu no suki na no yo.

B: Ikura "Teishu no suki na aka ebōshi" demo, anata made suru koto nai ja nai no!

A: My husband likes to put strawberry jam on his sashimi.

B: Heavens! I know they say "A husband's taste is also his wife's," but that doesn't mean you have to do the same!

OFF THE BEATEN PATH

Michi naranu koi 道ならぬ恋 Immoral love.

●➞ 彼女は夫も子供も捨てて、若い男と道ならぬ恋に走った。

Kanojo wa otto mo kodomo mo sutete, wakai otoko to michi naranu koi ni hashitta.

She left her husband and children and ran off with a younger man.

➥ 道ならぬ恋に落ちた温子は、親戚中から非難された。

Michi naranu koi ni ochita Atsuko wa, shinseki-jū kara hinan sareta.

Atsuko was criticized by all her relatives for her illicit affair.

Uwaki 浮気 (Lit., "floating *ki*") To cheat; to be unfaithful (to a spouse or lover).

➥ 彼はまた浮気がばれて、奥さんに家をたたき出された。

Kare wa mata uwaki ga barete, okusan ni ie o tatakidasareta.

His wife caught him cheating again and threw him out of the house.

➥ 浮気心を起こすと、ろくなことはない。

Uwaki-gokoro o okosu to, roku na koto wa nai.

No good can come of letting your eye wander.

Yoromeku よろめく (Lit., "stagger") To stray; to cheat; to be led astray; to be seduced into cheating.

➥ 婚約者がいるのにほかの男によろめくような女は、結婚してもきっと浮気するだろう。

Kon'yaku-sha ga iru no ni hoka no otoko ni yoromeku yō na onna wa, kekkon shite mo kitto uwaki suru darō.

Any woman who would let herself be seduced by a man other than her fiancé would surely be unfaithful after the marriage as well.

➥ あの暇な奥さんたちは、昼間のよろめきドラマを、真剣に見ている。

Ano hima na okusan-tachi wa, hiruma no yoromeki dorama o, shinken ni mite iru.

Housewives who have a lot of time on their hands take those daytime soaps about people's extramarital affairs pretty seriously.

Furin 不倫 (Lit., "non-ethics") An adulterous affair.

➥ 彼女は夫の浮気に腹を立て、自分も不倫をした。

Kanojo wa otto no uwaki ni hara o tate, jibun mo furin o shita.

Out of anger over her husband's infidelity, she had an affair herself.

➼ 彼女は上司との不倫がばれて、会社にいづらくなった。

Kanojo wa jōshi to no furin ga barete, kaisha ni izuraku natta.

It was hard for her to stay in the company after people found out she was having an affair with her supervisor.

Utsurigi 移り気 (Lit., "shifting *ki*") Fickle; changeable.

➼ 彼女は移り気だから、もう前の彼にあきて別の人と同棲している。

Kanojo wa utsurigi da kara, mō mae no kare ni akite betsu no hito to dōsei shite iru.

She's so fickle she's already gotten sick of her last boyfriend and is living with someone else now.

Asobi 遊び (Lit., "play") Casual sex; fooling around; irresponsible. lovemaking

➼ 彼は、「君とは遊びじゃない」と言っておきながら、私をさんざん弄んで捨てた男だ。

Kare wa, "Kimi to wa asobi ja nai" to itte okinagara, watashi o sanzan moteasonde suteta otoko da.

He's the one who assured me he was serious about our relationship, had some fun with me, and then dumped me.

➼ 彼とはほんの遊びのつもりだ。

Kare to wa hon no asobi no tsumori da.

I only think of him as a casual partner.

➼ 「遊びだよ」って最初から言っているでしょう！

"Asobi da yo" tte saisho kara itte iru deshō!

I told you from the beginning it was just for fun.

Hiasobi 火遊び (Lit., "playing with fire") Casual sexual encounters; indiscriminate casual sex.

➼ 友達と飲みに行き、酔った勢いで行きずりの男と火遊びを
してしまった。

Tomodachi to nomi ni iki, yotta ikioide yukizuri no otoko to hiasobi o shite shimatta.

I went drinking with some friends and got so drunk that I ended up doing it with some guy I'd only just met.

➼ 火遊びをするとやけどをするよ。

Hiasobi o suru to yakedo o suru yo.

If you play with fire, you're gonna get burned.

Okabore suru 岡惚れする (Lit., "hill infatuation") To secretly harbor feelings for another's spouse or lover.

➼ A: 「彼女、どうやらあなたのご主人に岡惚れしちゃったら
しいの」

B: 「物好きもいたもんね、のしつけて差し上げるわよ」

A: *Kanojo, dō yara anata no go-shujin ni okabore shichatta rashii no.*

B: *Monozuki mo ita mon ne, noshi tsukete sashiageru wa yo.*

A: It looks to me like she's got a thing for your husband.

B: No accounting for taste, is there? She can have him.
(⚓ *Noshi tsukete sashiageru* means, "I'd wrap [him] up with ribbons and give [him to her].")

Yoko-renbo suru 横恋慕する (Lit., "side love and longing") To be enamored of someone else's mate.

➼ 人の女房に横恋慕するとは不届きな奴だ。

Hito no nyōbō ni yoko-renbo suru to wa futodoki na yatsu da.

The guy's got a lot of nerve, falling in love with somebody's wife.

➼ 人の亭主に横恋慕なんかするから、泣くはめになるんだよ。

Hito no teishu ni yoko-renbo nanka suru kara, naku hame ni naru n' da yo.

You wouldn't be crying like this if you hadn't gone falling for some other woman's man.

Sankaku-kankei 三角関係 (Lit., "triangle relationship")

The eternal triangle; a love triangle; a love relationship complicated by the involvement of a third party.

❧ 友達の彼を好きになっちゃって、三角関係に悩んでいる。

Tomodachi no kare o suki ni natchatte, sankaku-kankei ni nayande iru.

I fell for my friend's boyfriend, and now I'm in this triangle situation that's really eating away at me.

❧ 彼らは三角関係のトラブルで警察沙汰になった。

Karera wa sankaku-kankei no toraburu de keisatsu-zata ni natta.

Their love triangle got so messy the police were finally called in.

One often hears that some unfortunate incident or other has occurred because of "an entanglement of affections." But why would affections get entangled? Only because they aren't properly balanced—one party feels more affection than the other, and that tips the scales. A slight imbalance can be overcome easily enough, but when you start talking "separation," it gets complicated. And of course when a "love rival" is involved, well, no good is likely to come of it all. This sort of trouble— trouble involving love and hatred—is something that humans through the ages, and in every culture, have found impossible to prevent or resolve. Perhaps our creators wanted it that way; perhaps it's all for their entertainment: one big soap opera for the gods.

PART 2

FROM UNCERTAINTY
TO HATE

AMBIVALENCE

Suki de mo kirai de mo nai 好きでも嫌いでもない

Neither like nor dislike; have no particular feelings about.

➾ 魚は好きでも嫌いでもないけれど、刺身は苦手だ。

Sakana wa suki de mo kirai de mo nai keredo, sashima wa nigate da.

I can take fish or leave it, but sashimi's definitely not for me.

➾ 男:「君、僕のこと嫌い？」
女:「別に好きでも嫌いでもないわ」
男:「よかった。じゃあ、いつか好きになる可能性もあるわけだ」
女:「嫌いになる可能性もね」

Otoko: Kimi, boku no koto kirai?
Onna: Betsu ni suki de mo kirai de mo nai wa.
Otoko: Yokatta. Jā, itsuka suki ni naru kanō-sei mo aru wake da.
Onna: Kirai ni naru kanō-sei mo ne.

He: Do you dislike me?
She: I don't particularly like you or dislike you.
He: That's good. It means in time you might learn to like me.
She: Yes, or *dis*like you.

Betsu ni 別に Not particularly; not really; nothing much.

➾ 父親:「あの相手はどうなんだ？」
娘:「別に好きでも嫌いでもないわ」
父親:「別にって言ったって、好きなんだろう？」
娘:「好き嫌いで付き合ってるんじゃないわよ」

Chichi-oya: Ano aite wa dō nan da?
Musume: Betsu ni suki de mo kirai de mo nai wa.
Chichi-oya: Betsu ni tte itta tte, suki nan darō?
Musume: Suki-kirai de tsukiatte 'ru n' ja nai wa yo.

Father: So how do you feel about that young man?
Daughter: I don't know. I don't feel all that strongly one way or another.

Father:　Come, come, now. You like him, right?

Daughter: Just because I'm going out with him doesn't mean I have strong feelings one way or the other!

He to mo omowanai　屁とも思わない　(Lit., "not feel a fart") To think nothing of; to not care about; to be completely indifferent to; to not give a damn.

•• A:「私の気持ち、彼ったら少しは分かってくれてもいいと思うんだけど」

B:「なにいってんのよ。あいつあんたのことなんか、屁とも思っていないわよ」

A: *Watashi no kimochi, kare ttara sukoshi wa wakatte kurete mo ii to omou n' da kedo.*

B: *Nani itte n' no yo. Aitsu anta no koto nanka, he to mo omotte inai wa yo.*

A: You'd think he'd try to have some understanding of how I feel.

B: What are you talking about? He couldn't care less about you."

•• 大介は約束を破ることなんか屁とも思わない奴だ。

Daisuke wa yakusoku o yaburu koto nanka he to mo omowanai yatsu da.

Daisuke thinks nothing of breaking a promise.

Ganchū ni nai　眼中にない　(Lit., not in one's eyes") To take no notice of; to disregard; to ignore; to consider [something or someone] beneath one's notice.

•• 友子がどんなに言い寄っても、良夫は彼女のことなんか眼中にない。

Tomoko ga donna ni iiyotte mo, Yoshio wa kanojo no koto nanka ganchū ni nai.

No matter how much Tomoko tries to entice him, Yoshio hardly knows she's alive.

FROSTY SILENCE

Mushi suru 無視する (Lit., "not see") To ignore; to disregard; to brush aside; to slight.

↦ 謝ろうと思っていたのに、彼女は無視して行ってしまった。

Ayamarō to omotte ita no ni, kanojo wa mushi shite itte shimatta.

I wanted to apologize, but she just ignored me and walked away.

↦ 彼女なんか大嫌い！徹底的に無視してやる！

Kanojo nanka daikirai! Tettei-teki ni mushi shite yaru!

I hate that woman! From now on I'm going to pretend she doesn't exist!

Soppo o muku そっぽをむく (Lit., "turn the other way") To turn or look away from; to ignore; to reject.

↦ いまどき親孝行の話をしても、若者はそっぽをむいて聞かないよ。

Imadoki oya-kōkō no hanashi o shite mo, wakamono wa soppo o muite kikanai yo.

Nowadays young folks just turn a deaf ear to the subject of filial piety.

↦ 温泉、カラオケ旅行の企画は若い社員にそっぽをむかれてしまった。やはり、グァム3泊ぐらいでなくちゃ駄目なのかなあ。

Onsen, karaoke ryokō no kikaku wa wakai shain ni soppo o mukarete shimatta. Yahari, Guamu sanpaku kurai de nakucha dame na no ka nā.

The younger staff members wouldn't even listen to the plans for staying at a hot spring or taking a karaoke tour. It looks like the company trip will have to be at least a three-night stay in Guam.

↦ 人と話す時はちゃんと相手の目を見て話しなさい。そっぽをむいて聞くなんて失礼だよ。

Hito to hanasu toki wa chanto aite no me o mite hanashi-nasai. Soppo o muite kiku nante shitsurei da yo.

When you're having a conversation with someone, look them right in the eyes. It's rude to look away when a person's talking.

Shiga ni mo kakenai 歯牙にもかけない (Lit., "not even hang on one's teeth") To pay no attention to; to act as if something or someone is beneath notice.

➼ A: 「スティーブったら、会社の女の子のことなんか歯牙にもかけないって態度とるのよね」
　　B: 「ほんと、ちょっとばかり親が金持ちだからってさ。こっちだってあんなマザコン男、願い下げよねえ」

A: Sutiibu ttara, kaisha no onna no ko no koto nanka shiga ni mo kakenai tte taido toru no yo ne.

B: Honto, chotto bakari oya ga kanemochi da kara tte sa. Kotchi datte anna mazakon otoko, negai-sage yo nē.

A: That damn Steve acts like the women in the company are totally beneath him.

B: I know. Just because his parents have a little money. Well, I for one can do without a mama's boy like that, anyhow.

➼ 彼女は仕事一筋で、言い寄る男たちを歯牙にもかけない。

Kanojo wa shigoto hitosuji de, iiyoru otokotachi o shiga ni mo kakenai.

She only cares about work and pays no attention to the guys who try to hit up on her.

Nibe mo nai にべもない (Lit., "no glue") Flat [refusal]; curt [reply]; blunt [retort].

➼ 赤十字の寄付をお願いしたら、うちは慈善事業はしていないと、にべもない返事をされた。

Seki-jūji no kifu o onegai shitara, uchi wa jizen-jigyō wa shite inai to, nibe mo nai henji o sareta.

When I asked her to donate to the Red Cross, she gave a curt reply, saying that her home was not a charity organization.

◆◆ 母親：「芳子、そんなにべもない断り方したら失礼なんじゃ
　　　　ないの？」
　　娘：　「いいの、あの人しつこいんだもの」

*Haha-oya: Yoshiko, sonna nibe mo nai kotowarikata shi-
　　　　　tara shitsurei nan ja nai no?*
Musume:　Ii no, ano hito shitsukoi n' da mono.

Mother:　Yoshiko, don't you think it's rude to be so blunt
　　　　　when you turn someone down?
Daughter: It's all right. The guy's being an absolute pest.

◆◆ 「悪いけど、これやってくれない？」と頼んだら、「それは私
の仕事ではない」とにべもなく断られた。

*"Warui kedo, kore yatte kurenai?" to tanondara, "Sore wa
watashi no shigoto de wa nai" to nibe mo naku kotowarareta.*

I asked him politely to do something for me, and he turned
me down flat, saying, "It's not my job."

Aite ni shinai 相手にしない To have nothing to do with;
to pay no attention to; to ignore

◆◆ A：「彼女はお高くとまっているね」
　　B：「そう、三高の逆はみんな相手にしないのよ」

A:　Kanojo wa otakaku tomatte iru ne.
B:　Sō, sankō no gyaku wa minna aite ni shinai no yo.

A:　She's pretty stuck-up, isn't she?
B:　Yep. She won't even look at a guy who isn't tall, rich,
　　and from a good university.

◆◆ あんなわがままな人は、相手にしないほうがいい。

Anna wagamama na hito wa, aite ni shinai hō ga ii.

You shouldn't have anything to do with somebody that
selfish.

◆◆ ジョンはとても穏やかで、だれかがけんかをしかけてきて
も、相手にしない。

*Jon wa totemo odayaka de, dare ka ga kenka o shikakete
kite mo, aite ni shinai.*

John is really mellow. If anybody tries to start a fight with him, he just ignores them.

Toritsuku shima mo nai とりつく島もない (Lit.,"no island to cling to") Won't listen to a word one says; won't give one a chance to talk or explain at all.

➣ 私が謝ろうとしても彼女はしらんぷりで、まったくとりつく島もない。

Watashi ga ayamarō to shite mo kanojo wa shiranpuri de, mattaku toritsuku shima mo nai.

When I try to apologize, she just blows me off. She won't listen to a word I say.

➣ あの人、ふだんやさしいけどいったん怒ったらとりつく島がなくなるわよ。

Ano hito, fudan yasashii kedo ittan okottara toritsuku shima ga naku naru wa yo.

She's usually nice but, boy, when she gets mad, forget it: there's no talking to her.

DERISION

Baka ni suru ばかにする (Lit., "make stupid") To make fun of; to be scornful of; to patronize; to make a fool of.

➣ 彼女は田舎者だと言って私をばかにした.

Kanojo wa inaka-mono da to itte watashi o baka ni shita.

She made fun of me, calling me a hick.

➣ 男:「売り上げのノルマが達成できないんだって？ 僕が手
　　伝ってあげようか？」
　女:「ばかにしないでよ！ だれがあんたの助けなんか、借
　　りるもんですか！」

Otoko: Uriage no noruma ga tassei dekinai n' datte? Boku ga tetsudatte ageyō ka?

Onna: Baka ni shinaide yo! Dare ga anta no tasuke nanka, kariru mon desu ka!

He: I hear you're not going to meet your sales quota. Want me to give you a hand?

She: Don't patronize me! Who the hell would ask you for help?

Hana de warau 鼻で笑う (Lit., "laugh with the nose") To snort derisively; to dismiss [someone's ability or worth] with an ironic laugh.

➡ 一人暮らしがしたいと言ったら、母に「ご飯ひとつ炊けないのに」と、鼻で笑われた。

Hitori-gurashi ga shitai to ittara, haha ni "Gohan hitotsu takenai no ni" to, hana de warawareta.

When I told her I wanted to live alone, my mother said mockingly, "Ha! You who can't even cook a pot of rice?"

Hana de ashirau 鼻であしらう (Lit., "handle [someone] by the nose") To turn up one's nose at; to look down upon.

➡ 求人募集をしている会社に履歴書を持って行ったら、「あなたではちょっと無理ですね」と鼻であしらわれた。

Kyūjin-boshū o shite iru kaisha ni rirekisho o motte ittara, "Anata de wa chotto muri desu ne" to hana de ashirawareta.

I took my resumé to a company that was recruiting people, but they just turned up their noses and said, "You're hardly qualified."

Sesera warau せせら笑う To sneer at; to laugh mockingly at; to smile scornfully at.

➡ 私の丹精込めて描いた絵を見て、彼はせせら笑って言った。「ま、君としてはこんなところが精一杯だろうな」

Watashi no tansei komete kaita e o mite, kare wa sesera waratte itta. "Ma, kimi to shite wa konna tokoro ga sei-ippai darō na."

He looked at the painting I'd worked so hard on, sneered and said, "Well, I suppose this is about as good an effort as you're capable of."

➼ 月100万でどうだと言ったら、他の会社は最低500万は出す
と言っていると、その会計士はせせら笑った。

Tsuki hyakuman de dō da to ittara, hoka no kaisha wa saitei gohyakuman wa dasu to itte iru to, sono kaikei-shi wa sesera waratta.

When I asked what he would think of a million yen a month, the accountant laughed scornfully and said other companies were offering him at least five million.

Gotoki ～ごとき -like; *that* sort of [person or thing] (a word implying deprecation of the person or thing named).

➼ 坂田ごときに負けられるか、あいつはハンデ15で、おれは
ゴルフ歴十年のベテランだぞ。

Sakata gotoki ni makerareru ka, aitsu wa hande-jūgo de, ore wa gorufu-reki jūnen no beteran da zo.

I can't lose to somebody like Sakata. He's got a handicap of fifteen, and I'm a veteran with ten years of golf behind me.

➼ 若手批評家ごときに私の深遠な文学がわかるはずがない。

Wakate hihyō-ka gotoki ni watashi no shinen na bungaku ga wakaru hazu ga nai.

I wouldn't expect some upstart young critic to understand the profundity of my literary works.

Kuchihodo ni mo nai 口ほどにもない (Lit., "Not as much as the mouth") A set phrase used to describe someone who talks big but isn't in fact capable of much.

➼ 柔道は黒帯だと自慢していたが、1回戦で負けてしまうとは、
あいつも口ほどにもないな。

Jūdō wa kuro-obi da to jiman shite ita ga, ikkai-sen de makete shimau to wa, aitsu mo kuchihodo ni mo nai.

He was bragging about being a black belt in judo, then he lost in the first match. He's obviously not as good as he'd like us to believe.

➼ 酒なら横綱級と聞いてきたが、おれより先に酔いつぶれる
とは口ほどにもない奴だ。

Sake nara yokozuna-kyū to kiite kita ga, ore yori saki ni yoitsubureru to wa kuchihodo ni mo nai yatsu da.

He said he was a world-class drinker, but I guess it was all talk. I drank him under the table.

ARROGANCE AND PRIDE

~kidori ～気取り (Lit., taking a *ki*") Pretending to be ~; passing oneself off as ~; acting like ~; pseudo-~; ~-manqué.

◆◇ 婚約しただけなのに、彼女はもう女房気取りで僕の世話をやきだした。

Kon'yaku shita dake na no ni, kanojo wa mō nyōbō-kidori de boku no sewa o yakidashita.

We're only engaged, but she's already started acting like the "little woman," nagging and fussing over me.

◆◇ たまたまCMで話題になったら、もう女優気取りでいる。

Tamatama shiemu de wadai ni nattara, mō jōyū-kidori de iru.

Just because she happened to appear in one popular TV commercial, she acts like she's a seasoned actress.

Tengu ni naru 天狗になる (Lit., "become a *tengu* [long-nosed goblin]") To be full of oneself; to be puffed up with pride; to let success go to one's head.

◆◇ あの作家は新人賞をとってから、すっかり天狗になったね。

Ano sakka wa shinjin-shō o totte kara, sukkari tengu ni natta ne.

That writer's been pretty pleased with herself since she won that prize for new authors.

◆◇ 彼は若くして横綱になったが、決して天狗にならず、稽古を怠らない。

Kare wa wakakushite yokozuna ni natta ga, kesshite tengu ni narazu, keido o okataranai.

Though he became a *yokozuna* [grand champion] while still young, it didn't go to his head; he never let up on his practice.

Ibaru いばる Act haughty; lord it over others; boast; swagger.

➡ ちょっとばかり出世したからって、いばるなんていやな奴だ。

Chotto bakari shusse shita kara tte, ibaru nante iya na yatsu da.

What a creep! He rises in the world the tiniest bit and starts to lord it over everybody.

➡ 彼女は、あんなに偉くなっても決していばったりしない。

Kanojo wa, anna ni eraku natte mo kesshite ibattari shinai.

As important as she's become, she never acts the least bit haughty.

Taka-bisha 高飛車 (Lit., "high-flying car") High-handed manner; offensively snobbish way [of speaking].

➡ 友人を訪ねて行ったら、秘書が「お約束のない方はお取り次ぎできません」と、えらく高飛車ゃに言いやがった。

Yūjin o tazunete ittara, hisho ga "oyakusoku no nai kata wa otoritsugi dekimasen" to, eraku taka-bisha ni iiyagatta.

I went to visit my friend, and his secretary gave me this incredibly snooty "We cannot admit anyone without an appointment."

➡ 何よ、あの高飛車ゃな断わり方、私はセールスに行ったんじゃないのよ。いい化粧品だからあなたもどう？と薦めただけなのよ。

Nani yo, ano taka-bisha na kotowarikata, watashi wa sērusu ni itta n' ja nai no yo. Ii keshōhin dakara anata mo dō? to susumeta dake na no yo.

What's with that high-handed attitude, anyway? She acts like I went there to sell her something, when all I did was tell her it was a good line of cosmetics and suggest that she might try it too.

Funzorikaeru ふんぞり返る   Act haughty; put oneself above others.

●● 最近出世した友達に会いに行ったら、ふんぞり返っていたので不愉快になった。

Saikin shusse shita tomodachi ni ai ni ittara, funzorikaette ita no de fuyukai ni natta.

I went to see this friend of mine who's been moving up in the world lately, but she acted so high and mighty it was really unpleasant.

●● 新しくきた専務は気さくな人で、専務の椅子にふんぞり返っていない。

Atarashiku kita senmu wa kisaku na hito de, senmu no isu ni funzorikaette inai.

The new managing director is just a regular guy; he doesn't try to throw his weight around.

Hana ni kakeru 鼻にかける   (Lit., "hang on one's nose") To be excessively proud of one's own or a family member's accomplishment.

●● あの人、アメリカの大学を出たことを鼻にかけているのよ、いけすかない奴。

Ano hito, America no daigaku o deta koto o hana ni kakete iru no yo, ikesukanai yatsu.

What a jerk—he thinks he's hot stuff because he graduated from an American university.

●● あいつ、コンクールに入賞したのを鼻にかけて、この頃生意気になったな。

Aitsu, konkūru ni nyūshō shita no o hana ni kakete, konogoro namaiki ni natta na.

Taking first prize in the competition went to his head, and he's been awfully snotty lately.

Hanamochi naranai 鼻持ちならない   To be unable to stand; to find unbearable. (⚠ Usually used to express distaste for arrogant, pompous behavior or people.)

➡ あの気取った話し方が鼻持ちならないと、広田先生は学生に人気がない。

Ano kidotta hanashikata ga hanamochi naranai to, Hirota-sensei wa gakusei ni ninki ga nai.

Professor Hirota isn't very popular with the students—they can't take his affected way of speaking.

➡ なんでもブランド品で身を固めた女は鼻持ちならない。

Nandemo burando-hin de mi o katameta onna wa hana-mochi naranai.

I can't stand women who drape themselves head to toe in designer clothes.

Taido ga dekai/taido ga ookii 態度がでかい/態度が大きい (Lit., "attitude is big") To cop an attitude; to think too much of oneself; to act more important than one's position warrants.

➡ 一流といわれる店は、ボーイまで態度でがでかいから行く気がしない。

Ichiryū to iwareru mise wa, bōi made taido ga dekai kara iku ki ga shinai.

I have no desire to go to what people call the "finest" restaurants, because in those places even the waiters have an attitude.

➡ あんなでかい態度でセールスに来たって、だれが買ってやるもんか。

Anna dekai taido de sērusu ni kita tte, dare ga katte yaru mon ka.

Who the heck would buy anything from a salesman who lords it over you like that?

Omoi-agari 思い上がり To have an undeservedly high opinion of oneself.

➡ 彼、みんなが言うことを聞くと思うなんて、思い上がってるよ。

Kare, minna ga iu koto o kiku to omou nante, omoi-agatte 'ru yo.

If he thinks everyone is going to listen to what he says, he must have an inflated opinion of himself.

➺ あの程度で、私たちと対等に仕事をしてるだなんて、彼女、思い上がりもはなはだしいんじゃないの？

Ano teido de, watashitachi to taitō ni shigoto o shite 'ru da nante, kanojo, omoi-agari mo hanahadashii n' ja nai no?

Imagine claiming that what little work she does puts her on a level with the rest of us—she must be totally delusional.

KNOWING NO SHAME

Atsukamashii　あつかましい　Nervy; audacious; fresh; cheeky; impudent.

➺ いくら友だちだって、いつもうちで夕飯を食べるなんてあつかましいわよ。

Ikura tomodachi datte, itsumo uchi de yūhan o taberu nante atsukamashii wa yo.

Sure he's a friend, but still, he's got some nerve always coming over to our place for dinner.

➺ 初対面で結婚してくれなんて随分あつかましい男だと思ったわよ。でも、結婚しちゃった。

Shotai-men de kekkon shite kure nante zuibun atsukamashii otoko da to omotta wa yo. Demo kekkon shichatta.

I thought he was awfully cheeky, proposing to me the first time we met. But I married him.

Zūzūshii　ずうずうしい　Nervy; cheeky; fresh; offhanded; presumptuous (not quite as severe as *atsukamashii*).

➺ 2日という約束なのに、彼女、ずうずうしくもう1週間もいるの。

Futsuka to iu yakusoku na no ni, kanojo, zūzūshiku mō isshū-kan mo iru no.

She was supposed to be here just two days, but she's had the brass to stay a week already.

➡ 隣の猫はずうずうしくて、家のソファーで昼寝していく。

Tonari no neko wa zūzūshikute, ie no sofā de hirune shite iku.

The cat from next door thinks nothing of taking a nap on our sofa before it leaves.

Tsura no kawa ga atsui 面の皮が厚い (Lit., "face skin is thick") Shameless; audacious; brazen; having a lot of nerve.

➡ 前に貸した金も返さないで、また借りに来るとは、お前も面の皮が厚いなあ。

Mae ni kashita kane mo kaesanaide, mata kari ni kuru to wa, omae mo tsura no kawa ga atsui nā.

You've got a lot of nerve, coming to me for another loan when you haven't paid back the last one.

➡ 「だれでもやっていることだ」とうそぶく面の皮の厚い汚職議員は面汚しだ。

"Dare de mo yatte iru koto da" to usoboku tsura no kawa no atsui oshoku-gi'in wa urayogoshi da.

Those shameless, bribe-sucking politicians who go around blustering about how "everybody does it" are such a disgrace.

Asamashii あさましい Wretched; mean; base; scumlike.

➡ A: 「彼って、いつも楽しくておいしいところだけ取ろうとするんだよね」
   B: 「ほんと、ハイエナみたいなあさましいやつ！」

A: Kare tte, itsumo tanoshikute oishii tokoro dake torō to suru n' da yo ne.
B: Honto, haiena mitai na asamashii yatsu!

A: He always tries to take center stage and get all the credit for everything.
B: I know. He's like a hyena or something—what a scumbag.

➡ 人の懐ばっかり当てにするなんて、あさましい人ね！

Hito no futokoro bakkari ate ni suru nante, asamashii hito ne!

What a lowlife—he always wants someone else to pay.

Chakkari shite iru ちゃっかりしている Opportunistic; freeloading. (🎵 Said [somewhat indulgently] of someone who's forever taking advantage of others' good will.)

↪ 私の友達はちゃっかりしていて、デパートの化粧品売り場でお化粧してもらう。

Watashi no tomodachi wa chakkari shite ite, depāto no keshō-hin uriba de okeshō shite morau.

My friend's always looking for freebies. She even has her makeup done at department stores.

↪ グレースは講義をさぼって、試験の前になると友達のノートをちゃっかり写させてもらって進級した。

Gurēsu wa kōgi o sabotte, shiken no mae ni naru to tomodachi no nōto o chakkari utsusasete moratte shinkyū shita.

Grace skipped class a lot but passed anyway, because she had the gall to copy her friends' notes right before exams.

Aita kuchi ga fusagaranai 開いた口がふさがらない (Lit., "the open mouth won't close") Dumbfounded; shocked; so scandalized that one is at a loss for words.

↪ 生活に困ったからではなく、遊ぶ金欲しさに強盗をしたというから、開いた口がふさがらない。

Seikatsu ni komatta kara de wa naku, asobu kane hoshisa ni gōtō shita to iu kara, aita kuchi ga fusagaranai.

He says he held up the place not because he was in financial straits but because he wanted some pocket money. I'm just dumbfounded by that.

↪ A: 「彼女に指輪貸したら無くされちゃったのよ。おまけに、『イミテーションだったんでしょ』なんて言うのよ」
B: 「まあ、ずうずうしい！開いた口がふさがらないわ」

A: Kanojo ni yubiwa kashitara nakusarechatta no yo. Omake ni "imitēshon datta n' desho" nante iu no yo.
B: Mā, zūzūshii! Aita kuchi ga fusagaranai wa.

A: So I lend her my ring and she loses it. Then, just to add insult to injury, she says, "Well, it was an imitation, right?"

B: What nerve! Unbelievable.

Hin ga nai/hin no nai 品がない/品のない (Lit.,"no class") Unrefined; vulgar (said of behavior or speech).

➼ そんな品のない食べ方しないで。

Sonna hin no nai tabekata shinaide.

Stop eating in that vulgar way.

➼ A: 「彼女のドレス、ちょっと肌の出しすぎじゃない？」
  B: 「そうね、結婚式の衣装としては品がないわね」

A: Kanojo no doresu, chotto hada no dashisugi ja nai?
B: Sō ne, kekkon-shiki no ishō to shite wa hin ga nai wa ne.

A: Isn't her dress a little too revealing?
B: I'll say. Hardly right for a wedding.

INGRATITUDE

On shirazu 恩知らず (Lit., "not knowing gratitude") Ingratitude; also, an ingrate.

➼ 困ったときだけ来てあとは知らん振りだなんて、とんだ恩知らずだ。

Komatta toki dake kite ato wa shiran-furi da nante, tonda on shirazu da.

To come to us only when you're in trouble and ignore us the rest of the time tells me just one thing: you have no sense of gratitude.

➼ さんざん人の意見を聞きにきたくせに、ちょっと成功したら全部自分のアイデアだなんて恩知らずな奴だ！

Sanzan hito no iken o kiki ni kita kuse ni, chotto seikō shitara zenbu jibun no aidea da nante on shirazu na yatsu da!

He comes to me all the time to ask my opinion and then when he has the slightest success he takes all the credit for the idea himself. Ungrateful bastard!

On o ada de kaesu 恩を仇で返す (Lit., "return a favor

with injury") To bite the hand that feeds you; to do something nasty to someone who has done you a good turn.

‣ A: 「彼ったら、あんなに世話になった人のお嬢さんを、だまして捨てたんだって！」

　 B: 「恩を仇で返すにもほどがあるよ」

A: Kare ttara, anna ni sewa ni natta hito no ojōsan o, damashite suteta n' da tte!

B: On o ada de kaesu ni mo hodo ga aru yo.

A: They say he deceived the daughter of the man who took such good care of him, and then dumped her.

B: I've heard of biting the hand that feeds you, but that's going a little too far.

Ushira ashi de suna o kakeru　後足で砂をかける

(Lit., "kick sand on [someone] with the back feet") To turn a favor someone has done for one into a problem for them; to dump on someone (the image comes from the way a cat or dog covers its feces with sand or dirt).

‣ 彼はさんざん世話になった恩師に後足で砂をかけるように、大学を辞めた。

Kare wa sanzan sewa ni natta onshi ni ushiro-ashi de suna o kakeru yō ni, daigaku o yameta.

By quitting college, he was dumping on the professor who'd done so much to help him.

Bachi-atari　罰当たり　Behavior so disrespectful or immoral that it might rightfully be punished by divine retribution; also, a person who engages in such behavior.

‣ 親に手をあげるような罰当たりはもう息子とは思わないから、今すぐ出て行け。

Oya ni te o ageru yō na bachi-atari wa mō musuko to wa omowanai kara, ima sugu dete ike.

How dare you raise a hand against your own father! You're no son of mine! Get out of this house this instant!

‣ 墓石に腰掛けるなんて罰当たりなこと、しちゃあだめだよ。

Hakaishi ni koshi-kakeru nante bachi-atari na koto, shichā dame da yo.

Don't sit on that gravestone! Do you want to get struck by lightning?

Dono tsura sagete どの面下げて (Lit., "bringing which face?") Imagine you've done something so terrible that most people in your shoes would hesitate to ever show their face again. But *you* show up looking nonchalant, as if nothing had happened at all. You would hardly blame people for thinking you rather audacious, and for using this expression about you.

Tsura (面), is, by the way, a rude word for "face."

➻ さんざん人に迷惑をかけた挙げ句、金までもって逃げて、いまさらどの面下げて帰ってきたんだ！

Sanzan hito ni meiwaku o kaketa ageku, kane made motte nigete, imasara dono tsura sagete kaette kita n' da!

After causing me all sorts of problems and even running off with my money, you dare to show your face back here again!

THE COLD SHOULDER

Tsumetai 冷たい Cold.

➻ 彼女は冷たい人間だ。

Kanojo wa tsumetai ningen da.

She's a cold person.

➻ 妹は恋人に冷たくされたと泣いている。

Imōto wa koibito ni tsumetaku sareta to naite iru.

My little sister was crying, saying her boyfriend had been acting cold toward her.

Tsurenai　つれない　Cold; coldhearted; unfeeling.

➡️ 「どこへ行くの？」って彼に聞いたのに「どこでもいいじゃないか」なんて、つれない返事！！

"Doko e iku no?" tte kare ni kiita no ni "Doko de mo ii ja nai ka" nante, tsurenai henji!!

I asked where he was going, and he said, "What's it to you?" How do you like that for a cold reply!

➡️ あれっきり電話もくれないなんて、つれない人ね。

Arekkiri denwa mo kurenai nante, tsurenai hito ne.

Talk about cold, not to have called me once since that time.

Hana mo hikkakenai　鼻も引っかけない　(Lit., "don't even get one's nose caught ") Have absolutely nothing to do with; ignore completely; do not give someone the time of day.

➡️ A:「彼女は、言い寄る男たちには鼻も引っかけないのよ」
　　B:「望みが高いってことなの？」

A: Kanojo wa, iiyoru otokotachi ni wa hana mo hikkake-nai yo.
B: Nozomi ga takai tte koto na no?

A: She completely ignores all the men who try to chat her up.
B: Why's that? High standards?

Ken mo hororo　けんもほろろ　Bluntly; coldly; brusquely; curtly (used to describe a manner of refusing a request).

➡️ 先生に就職の推薦状を書いてもらおうと頼みに行ったら、けんもほろろに断られた。

Sensei ni shūshoku no suisen-jō o kaite moraō to tanomi ni ittara, ken mo hororo ni kotowarareta.

I went to ask my professor to write a job recommendation for me, and he bluntly refused.

➡️ 兄:「ねえ、おこづかい余ってたらちょっと貸してくれよ」
　　妹:「だめ！」
　　兄:「そんな、けんもほろろな……」

Ani: *Nē, okozukai amattetara chotto kashite kure yo.*
Imōto: Dame!
Ani: *Sonna, ken mo hororo na …*

Older brother: Look, if you've got any of your allowance
                left over, would you lend it to me?
Kid sister: No way!
Older brother: Geez. So cold …

Chi mo namida mo nai　血も涙もない (Lit., "without blood or tears") Cruel; cold-blooded; inhumane.

↬ 生まれたばかりの赤ちゃんまで殺すなんて、血も涙もない
男だ。

*Umareta bakari no akachan made korosu nante, chi mo
namida mo nai otoko da.*

Killing a newborn baby—the guy's not even human!

↬ 三十年間もまじめに働いてきたのに突然首にするとは、ま
ったく血も涙もない会社だ。

*Sanjū-nenkan mo majime ni hataraite kita no ni totsuzen
kubi ni suru to wa, mattaku chi mo namida mo nai kaisha da.*

What are you, completely heartless? How can you fire me
just like that, after I've given you thirty years of honest
work?

Shiroi me de miru　白い目で見る (Lit., "look at with white eyes") To look at or treat someone coldly; to express disapproval with a glance.

↬ とかく世間は、前科者を白い目で見るものだ。

Tokaku seken wa, zenka-mono o shiroi me de miru mono da.

The world can be pretty unforgiving toward people with
criminal records.

↬ 彼は、自分のミスで試合に負けたので、チームメイトから
白い目で見られている。

*Kare wa, jibun no misu de shiai ni maketa no de, chiimu-
mēto kara shiroi me de mirarete iru.*

Since it was his mistake that cost them the game, his team-
mates are eyeing him coldly.

Ushiro yubi o sasu 後ろ指をさす (Lit., "point fingers from behind") Speak ill of someone behind their back.

➥ その一家は放火犯の家族だといって後ろ指をさされ、いたたまれなくなって夜逃げをした。

Sono ikka wa hōka-han no kazoku da to itte ushiro yubi o sasare, itatamarenaku natte yonige o shita.

People were always whispering about how they were the family of the arsonist. It got so bad that finally one night they just up and left town.

➥ 私はなにも後ろ指をさされるようなことはしていない。

Watashi wa nani mo ushiro yubi o sasareru yō na koto wa shite inai.

I've done nothing to be ashamed of.

Kuchisaganai 口さがない (Lit., "no mouth nature") Gossipy; critical; never [having] a good word to say about anyone.

➥ 娘の離婚を口さがない連中が噂のたねにしているのには耐えられない。

Musume no rikon o kuchisaganai renchū ga uwasa no tane ni shite iru no ni wa taerarenai.

I can't stand the way the gossips are spreading rumors about my daughter's divorce.

➥ 妻：「ご近所の奥さん達がね、お父さんのこと『万年平社員』だって。失礼ね」
　　夫：「口さがない連中の言うことなんか、気にするな」

Tsuma: Go-kinjo no okusan-tachi ga ne, otōsan no koto "mannen hira-shain" datte. Shitsurei ne.

Otto:　Kuchisaganai renchū no iu koto nanka, ki ni suru na.

Wife:　　All the wives in the neighborhood keep saying you're going nowhere fast at your office. Isn't that rude of them?

Husband: Don't let what those gossips say bother you.

Sore ga dō shita; da kara nan na no; sore de?
それがどうした/だから何なの/それで？

So what; what of it; what's your point? (᠓ These are all ways of putting the lid on someone's boasting or big talk. They suggest that what the other person was saying is run-of-the-mill, nothing special, no big deal.)

•• A: 「うちのおとうさん、こんど部長になったんだよ」
　　B: 「ふうん、だから何なの」

　　A: Uchi no otōsan, kondo buchō ni natta n' da yo.
　　B: Fūn, da kara nan na no.

　　A: My dad was made head of his department.
　　B: Yeah? So?

SCOWLING AND FROWNING

Mayu o hisomeru　眉をひそめる　To frown or scowl in response to something unpleasant.

•• 彼らは青年の傍若無人な行為に眉をひそめた。

Karera wa seinen no bōjaku-bujin na kōi ni mayu o hisometa.

They all scowled with distaste at the youth's insolent behavior.

•• 近頃の犯罪は、眉をひそめたくなるような残虐なものが多い。

Chikagoro no hanzai wa, mayu o hisometaku naru yō na zangyaku na mono ga ōi.

A lot of crime these days is disgustingly cruel.

Me ni amaru　目にあまる　(Lit., "too much for the eyes") A bit much; intolerable (used to describe behavior or situations too offensive to be overlooked).

•• 子供のいたずらが目にあまるので、厳重に親に注意した。

Kodomo no itazura ga me ni amaru no de, genjū ni oya ni chūi shita.

The child's mischief was getting out of hand, so we gave her parents a stern warning.

➼ 駅前の放置自転車が目にあまるので、区役所に撤去を求める電話をした。

Ekimae no hōchi jitensha ga me ni amaru no de, kuyaku-sho ni tekkyo o motomeru denwa o shita.

All the abandoned bicycles in front of the station got to be too much of an eyesore, so I called the Ward Office to request that they be removed.

Hana-jiromu 鼻白む (Lit., "one's nose turns white") To be offended; to register one's surprise and disapproval.

➼ 何時間も待たせて、一言の詫びもない彼の態度に鼻白む思いだった。

Nanji-kan mo matasete, ichigon no wabi mo nai kare no taido ni hana-jiromu omoi datta.

I was appalled by his attitude—he didn't even offer a word of apology after keeping me waiting for hours.

➼ アイドル歌手のわがままなふるまいには、いくらファンでもすっかり鼻白んでしまった。

Aidoru kashu no wagamama na furumai ni wa, ikura fan de mo sukkari hana-jironde shimatta.

Even his fans were offended by the famous singer's selfish behavior.

Hinshuku o kau ひんしゅくを買う (Lit., "invite a frown") To act in such a way as to invite censure; to behave scandalously.

➼ 彼はいつも酒ぐせが悪くて人のひんしゅくを買うようなことをする。

Kare wa itsumo sakeguse ga warukute hito no hinshuku o kau yō na koto o suru.

He always gets out of control when he drinks, and does something outrageous.

•• 葬式に厚化粧で現われ、彼女は参列者のひんしゅくを買った。

Sōshiki ni atsu-geshō de araware, kanojo wa sanretsu-sha no hinshuku o katta.

The mourners were scandalized by the woman who arrived at the funeral made up like a whore.

Mu-shinkei 無神経 (Lit., "no nerves") Insensitive; lacking in common courtesy.

•• 夜の10時にピアノの練習を始めるなんて、ずいぶん無神経な人だ。

Yoru no jūji ni piano no renshū o hajimeru nante, zuibun mu-shinkei na hito da.

To start practicing the piano at ten in the evening shows an amazing disregard for common courtesy.

•• 子供を亡くして悲しんでいる人に、自分の子供の話ばかりするなんて、無神経にもほどがある。

Kodomo o nakushite kanashinde iru hito ni, jibun no kodomo no hanashi bakari suru nante mu-shinkei ni mo hodo ga aru.

How insensitive can you get—blabbering on about her own kid to someone who's mourning the loss of a child.

Shaku ni sawaru しゃくにさわる (Lit., "touch one's passion") [Something] makes one angry; [something] pisses one off.

•• 全くしゃくにさわる雨だ！ せっかくの野球の試合が中止になったじゃないか。

Mattaku shaku ni sawaru ame da! Sekkaku no yakyū no shiai ga chūshi ni natta ja nai ka.

This rain really pisses me off! The baseball game I've been looking forward to is cancelled!

•• 子どものくせにあんまり生意気なことを言うので、しゃくにさわってつい怒鳴ってしまった。

Kodomo no kuse ni anmari namaiki na koto o iu no de, shaku ni sawatte tsui donatte shimatta.

The kid comes out with such impudent things that it finally really got to me, and I wound up screaming at him at the top of my lungs.

Jōdan ja nai; jōdan deshō 冗談じゃない/冗談でしょう

Jōdan ja nai is often used quite lightly, to mean "Are you kidding?" But it can also be used more seriously, to express actual indignation at something unreasonable or unforgivable.

Jōdan deshō is a similar phrase that can also be used in both ways. When pronounced gruffly, it means "This is not a joking matter," and encourages the other person to reflect on the inappropriateness of a flippant remark.

➡ 妻に逃げられたんじゃないかって？　冗談じゃない、妻はお産で病院だよ。

Tsuma ni nigerareta n' ja nai ka tte? Jōdan ja nai, tsuma wa osan de byōin da yo.

Did my wife leave me? Don't be absurd. She's in the hospital having a baby.

➡ うちの犬がお宅の庭を荒らしたって？　冗談じゃないよ。いつもつないであるんだから。

Uchi no inu ga otaku no niwa o arashita tte? Jōdan ja nai yo. Itsumo tsunaide aru n' da kara.

You're saying that our dog messed up your yard? That's not possible. He's always chained up.

➡ えっ！　ぼくが金持ちだって？　冗談でしょう、誰がそんなこと言ったんだろう？

E! Boku ga kanemochi da tte? Jōdan deshō, dare ga sonna koto itta n' darō?

What? Me, a rich guy? That's a laugh. Who told you that, anyway?

SARCASM AND BULLYING

Iyami o iu 嫌味を言う To say something sarcastic or just plain nasty; to say something that's meant to hurt.

➥ 田中さんは遅刻が多いので「君のうちの方は時差があったっけ」と課長に嫌味を言われた。

Tanaka-san wa chikoku ga ōi no de "Kimi no uchi no hō wa jisa ga atta kke" to kachō ni iyami o iwareta.

Tanaka-san is often late, so the head of the section asked sarcastically if his home was in a different time zone.

➥ ほんとうにあの野郎は嫌味ばかり言う奴だ。

Hontō ni ano yarō wa iyami bakari iu yatsu da.

He's really a nasty bastard.

Atekosuru 当てこする To slam someone indirectly; to make an oblique, sarcastic remark; to slip in a sly dig at someone; to sarcastically drop a hint.

➥ 妹が私の服をよく無断で着て行くので、「あら、また新しい服を買ったの」と当てこすってやった。

Imōto ga watashi no fuku o yoku mudan de kite iku no de, "Ara, mata atarashii fuku o katta no" to atekosutte yatta.

My sister always borrows my clothes without my permission. Last time, I said to her, sarcastically, "Oh, did you get some new clothes?"

Iyagarase o suru 嫌がらせをする To harass; to intentionally upset or offend.

➥ 最近夜中に何度も無言電話がかかってくるのよ。誰かが嫌がらせをしているんだわ。

Yonaka ni nando mo mugon-denwa ga kakatte kuru no yo. Dare ka ga iyagarase o shite iru n' da wa.

Lately I get these phone calls in the middle of the night where the person doesn't say anything. Somebody's harassing me.

➥ 女の子：「ママ、文治くんが、私に嫌がらせばっかりするの！」
母親：　「きっと、あなたのことが好きなのよ。」
女の子：「そうかしら……」

Onna no ko: Mama, Fumiharu-kun ga, watashi ni iyagarase bakkari suru no!

Haha-oya: Kitto, anata no koto ga suki nano yo.

Onna no ko: Sō kashira ...

Girl:　　Mama, Fumiharu-kun is always doing rotten
things to me!

Mother:　That must mean he has a crush on you.

Girl:　　Really?

Iji ga warui 意地が悪い (Lit., "bad disposition") Mean; ill-
tempered.

➥ どうして彼って私に意地悪ばっかりするんだろう。

Dōshite kare tte watashi ni ijiwaru bakkari suru n' darō.

I wonder why he's always so mean to me.

➥ 意地悪！こんなに私が頼んでるのに！

Ijiwaru! Konna ni watashi ga tanonde 'ru no ni!

You're rotten! Can't you see I'm begging you?

Ijimeru いじめる To bully; to pick on; to torment.

➥ 子供の頃よく君にはいじめられたよ。

Kodomo no koro yoku kimi ni wa ijimerareta yo.

You bullied me a lot when we were kids, you know.

➥ みんなにいじめられるから、学校へ行きたくない！

Minna ni ijimerareru kara, gakkō e ikitakunai!

I don't want to go to school. Everybody picks on me there!

FINDING FAULT

Nankuse o tsukeru/ichamon o tsukeru 難癖をつける/
いちゃもんをつける To find fault with; to criticize.

➥ 人のすることに、いちいち難癖をつけるのはやめてよ！

Hito no suru koto ni, ichi-ichi nankuse o tsukeru no wa yamete yo!

Will you stop criticizing every single thing I do!

➥ あの客は、いつもうちの商品に、ああだこうだと難癖をつけては値切ろうとする。

Ano kyaku wa, itsumo uchi no shōhin ni, ā da kō da to nankuse o tsukete wa negirō to suru.

That particular customer is always finding something or other wrong with the merchandise and trying to get us to lower the prices.

➥ サラリーマン：（電車の中）「おい、いま足踏んだろ」
ちんぴら：　　　「なんだよ、俺にいちゃもんつけようってえのか？」

Sarariiman: (densha no naka) Oi, ima ashi fundarō.
Chinpira:　　Nanda yo, ore ni ichamon tsukeyō ttē no ka?

Businessman:　(on the train) Hey, you just stepped on my foot.
Gangster punk: Yeah? You got a problem with that?

Mekujira o tateru 目くじらを立てる (Lit., "raise the outer corners of the eyes") To raise one's eyebrows; to express disapproval (usually for a minor fault or error).

➥ 順子は、あれくらいのことで目くじらを立てるんだから、まったく人間が小さいよ。

Junko wa, are kurai no koto de mekujira o tateru n' da kara, mattaku ningen ga chiisai yo.

It's awfully small of Junko to attack a person over something so insignificant.

➥ ちょっとのことにも目くじらを立てるのが、君の悪いくせだよ。

Chotto no koto ni mo mekujira o tateru no ga, kimi no warui kuse da yo.

You have a bad habit of criticizing people for little things.

Hinan suru 非難する To criticize; to censure; to blame; to reproach; to denounce.

➻ あんな生意気な態度をとれば、非難されるのも無理はないよ。

Anna namaiki na taido o toreba, hinan sareru no mo muri wa nai yo.

You act so cocky it's no wonder they criticize you.

➻ 大臣は、暴言を吐いて非難ごうごうだった。

Daijin wa, bōgen o haite hinan gōgō datta.

The cabinet minister was generally denounced for those outrageous remarks.

Nonoshiru ののしる To yell at; to abuse someone; to call [someone] names.

➻ 彼女は、私が彼を奪ったと汚い言葉でののしった。

Kanojo wa, watashi ga kare o ubatta to kitanai kotoba de nonoshitta.

She was cursing at me right and left, accusing me of stealing her boyfriend.

➻ 彼は、リーにどんなにののしられても、決して言い訳をしなかった。

Kare wa, Rii ni donna ni nonoshirarete mo, kesshite iiwake o shinakatta.

No matter how much Lee yelled at him, he didn't make any excuses.

Batō suru 罵倒する To denounce; to [shower with] abuse; to heap abuse on; to curse; to rail at; to rake [someone] over the coals.

➻ 彼は、私を裏切り者だと罵倒した。

Kare wa, watashi o uragirimono da to batō shita.

He cursed me, saying I'd stabbed him in the back.

➻ あのぐらいのミスで罵倒することないのに。

Ano gurai no misu de batō suru koto nai no ni.

For a little mistake like that, there's no need to rake me over the coals.

Tataku 叩く (Lit., "hit") To lambaste; to blast; to criticize; to denounce. (⚘ Most commonly used in the passive voice, *tatakareru*.)

➡ 首相の発言は相手国に対して不穏当だと、マスコミに叩かれた。

Shushō no hatsugen wa aite-koku ni taishite fu-ontō da to, masukomi ni tatakareta.

The media blasted the prime minister, saying his statement was unfair to the other country.

➡ 彼の演出は批評家からさんざん叩かれました。

Kare no enshutsu wa hihyō-ka kara sanzan tatakaremashita.

The critics savaged his production [of the play].

Kotenpan ni yaru こてんぱんにやる To give [someone] hell; to really let [someone] have it; to beat [someone] to a [bloody] pulp; to beat [criticize] without mercy.

➡ A:「どうだった、今度の絵？」
　　B:「だめだ。構図が悪い、色使いがきたない、独創的じゃないって、こてんぱんに言われちゃった」

A: Dō datta, kondo no e?
B: Dame da. Kōzu ga warui, iro-zukai ga kitanai, dokusō-teki ja nai tte, kotenpan ni iwarechatta.

A: How did your latest painting go over?
B: It was a disaster. They said the composition was no good, the use of color was sloppy, the concept lacked originality—basically they tore me to pieces.

➡ 今日の野球は雪辱戦だったのに、またしてもこてんぱんにやられたよ。

Kyō no yakyū wa setsujoku-sen datta no ni, matashitemo kotenpan ni yarareta yo.

Today's baseball game was a rematch, but we got trounced again.

GETTING MAD

Mukatsuku むかつく To get angry; find offensive; feel disgusted; make one sick

•• あいつの生意気な態度、ほんとにむかつくんだよ！

Aitsu no namaiki na taido, honto ni mukatsuku n' da yo!

That smart-alecky attitude of his makes me sick!

•• A: 「山田のやつ、すぐひとりだけいい子になろうとするんだよね」

　　B: 「ほんと、あいつむかつくよな」

A: Yamada no yatsu, sugu hitori dake ii ko ni narō to suru n' da yo ne.

B: Honto, aitsu mukatsuku yo na.

A: Yamada's always playing the good little boy, isn't he?

B: I know, he's really disgusting.

Atama ni kuru 頭に来る (Lit., "comes to the head") To get angry; to get pissed off; to get mad.

•• 彼女が私の悪口を言いふらしていると聞いて、頭に来た。

Kanojo ga watashi no waruguchi o iifurashite iru to kiite, atama ni kita.

It pissed me off to hear she was going around bad-mouthing me.

•• A: 「もう頭に来る！　買ったばかりのスカートにコーヒーこぼされちゃった」

　　B: 「クリーニング代、ちゃんともらった？」

A: Mō atama ni kuru! Katta bakari no sukāto ni kōhii kobosarechatta.

B: Kuriiningu-dai, chanto moratta?

A: I'm so mad! Somebody spilled coffee on the skirt I just bought!

B: You got them to pay for the cleaning, I hope?

Katto suru/naru かっとする/なる To become suddenly angry; to flare up with anger; to fly into a rage.

➡ 彼は弱点を指摘されて、かっとした。

Kare wa jakuten o shiteki sarete, katto shita.

He blew his stack when they pointed out his shortcomings.

➡ 彼女は、かっとなりやすい性格なのでみんな敬遠している。

Kanojo wa, katto nariyasui seikaku na no de minna keien shite iru.

Everyone gives her a wide berth because she's so hot-tempered.

Ikari o kau/ikari ni fureru 怒りをかう/怒りに触れる
(Lit., "invite anger/touch anger") To make [someone] angry; to infuriate.

➡ 暴言を吐いた代議士は、有権者の怒りをかった。

Bōgen o haita daigishi wa, yūken-sha no ikari o katta.

The Diet member's outlandish remarks angered the voters.

➡ その銀行員は、あまりにも失礼な態度を取ったので客の怒りに触れた。

Sono ginkō-in wa, amari ni mo shitsurei na taido o totta no de kyaku no ikari ni fureta.

That bank clerk was so rude he made the customers angry.

Gekirin ni fureru 逆鱗に触れる
(Lit., "touch the backwards scales [of a dragon]") To enrage someone in a position of authority; to incur the wrath of a big shot. (⚓ It's said in Japan that the scales beneath a dragon's chin grow in a different direction, and that if you touched those scales, the dragon would become enraged and kill you. The term is now rather antiquated.)

➡ A: 「彼、部長に食ってかかって、逆鱗に触れたらしいよ」
　　B: 「あんなに穏やかな部長を怒らせるなんて、よほどのことを言ったんだね」

A: Kare, buchō ni kutte kakatte, gekirin ni fureta rashii yo.
B: Anna ni odayaka na buchō o okoraseru nante, yohodo no koto o itta n' da ne.

A: He lashed out at the department head and now he's really in hot water.

B: He must've said something pretty extreme, to piss off a guy who's that mild-mannered.

❧ あのドラ息子とうとう親父の逆鱗に触れて、家を追い出されたよ。

Ano dora-musuko tōtō oyaji no gekirin ni furete, ie o oi-dasareta yo.

Their good-for-nothing son finally did something that was just the last straw, and his father threw him out of the house.

Gekido suru 激怒する Wild rage; fury.

❧ 厚生省の汚職事件に国民は激怒した。

Kosei-shō no oshoku-jiken ni kokumin wa gekido shita.

The people were up in arms over the corruption scandal involving the Ministry of Health and Welfare.

❧ 激怒のあまり、父は身をふるわせた。

Gekido no amari, chichi wa mi o furuwaseta.

Dad was so full of rage he was shaking.

Yatsuatari suru 八つ当たりする (Lit., "eight hits")

Venting one's anger or frustration indiscriminately; snapping [lashing out] at anyone who happens to be around.

❧ ミカ、彼氏にふられたからって、ミーちゃんを蹴飛ばすことないでしょ。猫に八つ当たりしてどうするの。

Mika, kareshi ni furareta karatte, Miichan o ketobasu koto nai deshō. Neko ni yatsuatari shite dō suru no.

Mika, just because your boyfriend dumped you, you don't have to kick Mi-chan. It won't do any good to take it out on a cat.

❧ おい、今課長の所に行くとまずいぞ。進藤がミスして怒鳴られて、おれまでついでに怒られてさ、八つ当たりもいいところさ。

Oi, ima kachō no tokoro ni iku to mazui zo. Shindō ga misu shite donararete, ore made tsuide ni okorarete sa, yatsu-atari mo ii tokoro sa.

Hey, I wouldn't advise you to go see the section chief right now. He was yelling at Shindo for screwing up, and afterwards gave me hell for no reason. He's madder than a jar full of hornets.

(❀ *Mo ii tokoro* is a set phrase meaning totemo or sugoku. *Samui mo ii* tokoro means *Totemo samui* [it's cold as hell/it's very cold].)

ALL WORKED UP

Okanmuri おかんむり (Lit., "crown") Be cross; be ticked off; be put out.

Punpun okoru/puripuri okoru ぷんぷん怒る/ぷりぷり怒る Be in a huff; be furious; be indignant.

Kankan ni natte komaru かんかんになって怒る Hit the ceiling; fly off the handle; fly into a rage; see red; get angry.

Kannin bukuro no o ga kireru 堪忍袋の緒が切れる (Lit., "the cord on the patience bag breaks") Lose one's temper; run out of patience.

Iro o nasu 色をなす Turn red with anger; become indignant; flare up; get angry.

Aosuji o tatete okoru 青筋を立てて怒る (Lit., "get angry with veins standing out on forehead") Turn blue with rage; lose it completely.

Ikari shintō ni hassuru 怒り心頭に発する (Lit., "discharge an angry heart through the head") fly into a rage; go ballistic.

Harawata ga niekuri kaeru 腸(はらわた)が煮えくり返る (Lit., "the guts boil") To boil with rage; go into a boiling rage.

Atama kara yuge o tatete okoru 頭から湯気を立てて怒る (Lit., "get angry with steam rising from one's head") To blow one's top; to get really steamed; to boil with rage.

Dohatsu-ten o tsuku 怒髪天を衝く (Lit., "anger-hair points to heaven") To be infuriated; to be beside oneself with rage; to be transported with rage.

FED UP

Unzari suru うんざりする To have had one's fill of something unpleasant; to be fed up with; to be bored with; to be tired of.

➾ 彼の自慢話にはうんざりだ。

Kare no jiman-banashi ni wa unzari da.

I'm fed up with his bragging.

➾ あんな嫉妬深い女にはもううんざりだ。

Anna shitto-bukai onna ni wa mō unzari da.

I've had it up to here with her jealousy.

Akiru 飽きる To be sick of; to be tired of.

➾ A: 「ああ、もう女なんかたくさんだよ。飽きちゃった」
B: 「それ、一度いってみたかったんだろ？」

A: Ā, mō onna nanka takusan da yo. Akichatta.
B: Sore, ichido itte mitakatta n' daro?

A: Man, I've had enough of women. I'm sick to death of them.
B: I bet you've always wanted to say that, just once.

➾ そのせりふ、いい加減聞き飽きたよ。

Sono serifu, ii kagen kiki-akita yo.

I'm so tired of hearing that same old line.

➾ 彼女は飽きっぽいのでしょっちゅう恋人を変える。

Kanojo wa akippoi no de shotchū koibito o kaeru.

She loses interest easily and is always finding some new lover.

Uttōshii うっとうしい Tiresome; irksome; annoying.

➼ デートのたびに母に根掘り葉掘り聞かれるのは、うっとうしくてたまらない。

Dēto no tabi ni haha ni nehori-hahori kikareru no wa, uttōshikute tamaranai.

It's annoying, how inquisitive my mother gets every time I have a date.

➼ 彼女はどこにでもついて来たがるので、少々うっとうしい。

Kanojo wa doko ni de mo tsuite kitagaru no de, shōshō uttōshii.

She wants to tag along with me everywhere, and it gets a bit tiresome.

Urusai うるさい Noisy; also, strict; particular (used to describe [with annoyance] someone's strictness or particularity).

➼ ちょっと、そこの人、うるさいよ。静かにして。

Chotto, soko no hito, urusai yo. Shizuka ni shite.

Hey, you. Hold it down, will you?

➼ 料理にうるさい人との食事は嫌だ。魚には白ワイン、肉には赤だとか……

Ryōri ni urusai hito to no shokuji wa iya da. Sakana wa shiro-wain, niku wa aka da to ka ...

I hate eating dinner with people who are overly particular about their food. White wine with fish, red wine with meat ...

➼ 世話好きな叔母は私の顔を見ると、早く結婚しろと、うるさく言う。

Sewa zuki na oba wa watashi no kao o miru to, hayaku kekkon shiro to, urusaku iu.

My busybody aunt no sooner sees my face than she starts harping on me to get married.

Yakamashii やかましい Very noisy; very strict; very particular (similar to *urusai*, but stronger; used to describe a person whose strictness is such that failure to adjust to it may have unpleasant consequences).

➳ 父が門限にやかましかったので、いつも9時までに帰らなければならず大変だった。

Chichi ga mongen ni yakamashikatta no de, itsumo kuji made ni kaeranakereba narazu taihen datta.

My father was strict about my curfew. I always had to get home by nine, which was a big pain.

➳ 祖母は礼儀作法にやかましい人だった。

Sobo wa reigi-sahō ni yakamashii hito datta.

My grandmother was a fanatic about etiquette.

Utomashii うとましい Disagreeable; unpleasant; a drag; a pain in the ass.

➳ きっぱり別れたはずなのに、彼女に未練がましくされてうとましい限りだ。

Kippari wakareta hazu na no ni, kanojo ni miren gamashiku sarete utomashii kagiri da.

As far as I was concerned, we'd made a clean break. But she won't let it go, which is getting to be a serious pain in the ass.

➳ あばたもえくぼというけれど、逆にいやとなったら相手の優しささえうとましくなる

Abata mo ekubo to iu keredo, gyaku ni iya to nattara aite no yasashisa sae utomashiku naru.

They say when you fall in love even a person's warts look like beauty marks. But, on the other hand, once you stop loving them, even their good points start to seem like a drag.

Heki-eki suru 辟易する To have had more than enough of someone's persistent pestering; to not know how to handle someone's unwelcome interest.

➳ 隣の奥さんの質問責めには、いいかげん辟易している。

Tonari no okusan no shitsumon-zeme ni wa, ii kagen heki-eki shite iru.

I've had enough of the way the woman next door keeps grilling me.

•• 好きでもない女性のプレゼント攻勢には辟易する。

Suki de mo nai josei no purezento kōsei ni wa heki-eki suru.

A guy never knows what to do when a woman he isn't even interested in keeps sending him presents.

Hana ni tsuku 鼻につく (Lit., "sticks in the nose") To be sick of; to be fed up with; [something] gets on one's nerves.

•• 最初はかわいいと思った彼女の甘ったれた声も、このごろは鼻についてきた。

Saisho wa kawaii to omotta kanojo no amattareta koe mo, konogoro wa hana ni tsuite kita.

At first I thought that syrupy voice of hers was cute, but now I'm getting sick of it.

•• 彼の自慢話、いいかげん鼻につくよね。

Kare no jiman-banashi, ii kagen hana ni tsuku yo ne.

His boasting really gets on your nerves after a while.

Aiso o tsukasu 愛想をつかす (Lit., "exhaust love") To fall out of love with someone; to give up on someone one once loved.

•• 彼女は、ギャンブル好きの夫に愛想をつかして、実家に帰ってしまった。

Kanojo wa, gyanburu-zuki no otto ni aiso o tsukashite, jikka ni kaette shimatta.

She finally gave up on her husband, who had a problem with gambling, and went home to her parents.

•• あんなわがままな女、ほとほと愛想がつきたよ。

Anna wagamama na onna, hotohoto aiso ga tsukita yo.

I've had it up to here with that selfish bitch.

Iya ni naru いやになる To come to dislike; to hate; [something] makes one sick.

➨ 人間関係が煩わしくて、今の職場がいやになった。

Ningen-kankei ga wazurawashikute, ima no shokuba ga iya ni natta.

Dealing with the people there is such a drag I've come to hate the place where I work now.

➨ 結婚前は、いやになるくらい彼女に手紙を書いたものだ。

Kekkon-mae wa, iya ni naru kurai kanojo ni tegami o kaita mono da.

Before we were married, I wrote her enough letters to make anybody sick.

Shitsukoi しつこい Overly persistent; stubborn; pestering.

➨ 好きな人がいるからとはっきり断ったのに、あの人ったら、食事に行こうとか飲みに行こうとかしつこくて。

Suki na hito ga iru kara to hakkiri kotowatta no ni, ano hito ttara, shokuji ni ikō to ka nomi ni ikō to ka shitsukokute.

I said no and made it very clear that there was someone else, but he keeps pestering me to go out for a meal, or go out drinking or whatever.

➨ 彼は忘れっぽいから、何度でもしつこく注意しなければならない。

Kare wa wasureppoi kara, nando de mo shitsukoku chūi shinakereba naranai.

His memory's not so good, so I have to keep on warning him over and over again.

Kudoi くどい To repeatedly state the obvious.

➨ くどいな、同じ話なんどもするなよ。

Kudoi na, onaji hanashi nando mo suruna yo.

Enough already—we've heard that story a million times!

➨ 息子の自慢話をくどくど聞かされて辟易したよ。

Musuko no jiman-banashi o kudokudo kikasarete heki-eki shita yo.

I got so sick of hearing all the time about how great his son was.

Nechinechi ネチネチ Tedious, captious; carping [speech].

→ いつまでもネチネチ言われるより、いっそ、大声で叱られた方がさっぱりする

Itsumademo nechinechi iwareru yori, isso, ōgoe de shika-rareta hō ga sappari suru.

I'd rather have someone yell at me and get it over with than always be carping away at me like that.

→ ゴミを出す日を間違えたら、大家にネチネチと嫌味を言われた。

Gomi o dasu hi o machigaetara, ōya ni nechinechi to iyami o iwareta.

When I put the garbage out on the wrong day, I thought the landlady was never going to let me hear the end of it.

Osekkai おせっかい Meddling; unwelcome help [advice].

→ 子供は自分でやりたがっているのに、親が手を出すのは、いらぬおせっかいだ。

Kodomo ga jibun de yaritagatte iru no ni, oya ga te o dasu no wa, iranu osekkai da.

It must be a bummer for the kid: he wants to do it himself, but his old man keeps butting in.

→ 親切の押し売りは、単なるおせっかいだ。

Shinsetsu no oshiuri wa, tannaru osekkai da.

Trying too hard to be helpful—even if a person's intentions are good—is still a pain in the neck.

CANNOT STAND

Kirai/kirau 嫌い/嫌う To dislike; to hate; to despise; to loathe.

→ 彼は、やよいが嫌いだ。

Kare wa, Yayoi ga kirai da.

He despises Yayoi.

➡ 彼女はクラスの嫌われ者だ。

Kanojo wa kurasu no kirawaremono da.

The whole class hates her.

➡ A: 「どうしてあいつのことそんなに嫌うんだ」
　　B: 「『嫌いなものは嫌い』ってだけ」

A: Dōshite aitsu no koto sonna ni kirau n' da.
B: "Kirai na mono wa kirai" tte dake.

A: Why do you have to hate him so much?
B: I hate what I hate, that's all.

Kegirai suru 毛嫌いする (Lit., "hate with the hair") To feel [instinctual] repulsion towards; to be prejudiced against; to feel antipathy for.

➡ 彼は彼女を毛嫌いしていて、近寄るのを避けている。

Kare wa kanojo o kegirai shite ite, chikayoru no o sakete iru.

He just can't stomach the girl, and avoids being around her.

➡ そんなに彼のことを毛嫌いしないで、一度話でもしてみたら？

Sonna ni kare no koto o kegirai shinaide, ichido hanashi de mo shite mitara?

Why don't you stop being so prejudiced against him, and try talking to him once?

Ikesukanai いけすかない Creepy; unpleasant.

➡ あいつはえらぶって嫉妬深くて、いけすかない奴だ。

Aitsu wa erabutte shitto-bukakute, ikesukanai yatsu da.

He's self-important and jealous—an altogether unpleasant fellow.

➡ なによ！　気取っちゃって、いけすかない奴！

Nani yo! Kidotchatte, ikesukanai yatsu!

Who the hell do you think you are, you stuck-up bastard!

Mushi ga sukanai 虫が好かない Hard to like; unlikable.

⇴ 今度隣に越してきた夫婦は、どうも虫が好かない。

Kondo tonari ni koshite kita fūfu wa, dōmo mushi ga sukanai.

There's something I just don't like about the new couple who moved in next door.

⇴ あの男、なんだかきざったらしくて、虫が好かない。

Ano otoko, nandaka kizattarashikute, mushi ga sukanai.

That guy's not for me—there's something too affected about him.

Hanatsumami **鼻つまみ** (Lit., "nose pincher") [One who is] widely disliked; a nuisance; a pariah.

⇴ 彼女は噂好きのトラブルメーカーで、近所の鼻つまみになっている。

Kanojo wa uwasazuki no toraburumēkā de, kinjo no hanatsumami ni natte iru.

Nobody likes her: she's the neighborhood gossip and troublemaker.

⇴ 彼は酒癖が悪くてよく暴れるので、宴会の鼻つまみだ。

Kare wa sakeguse ga warukute yoku abareru no de, enkai no hanatsumami da.

He's a rotten, violent drunk—always the death of the party.

Iya de iya de tamaranai **いやでいやでたまらない** Hate [someone or something] so much one can't bear it; [something] drives one mad; [something] makes one want to scream.

⇴ 彼、しょっちゅう電話をかけてくるんだけど、私はあの人のこと、いやでいやでたまらないんです！

Kare, shotchū denwa o kakete kuru n' da kedo, watashi wa ano hito no koto, iya de iya de tamaranai n' desu!

He calls me all the time, and I can't stand him.

⇴ 私は、彼のねちねちしたしゃべりかたがいやでいやでたまらない。

Watashi wa, kare no nechinechi shita shaberikata ga iya de iya de tamaranai.

The tedious, droning way he talks drives me straight up the wall.

Iya yo iya yo mo suki no uchi いやよいやよも
好きのうち ("She says 'no,' but means come on'")

A: 「彼女、手を握ろうとしたら『いや』って言うんだよ。
『いやよいやよも好きのうち』ってことかな」

B: 「ばか。彼女の場合は、『いや』と言ったら、ほんと
におしまいだよ。だって、僕が経験者だもの。彼女
に振られたことがあるんだから」

A: *Kanojo, te o nigirō to shitara, "iya," tte iu n' da yo.
"Iya yo iya yo mo suki no uchi" tte koto ka na.*

B: *Baka. Kanojo no bāi wa, "iya" to ittara, honto ni
oshimai da yo. Datte, boku ga keiken-sha da mono.
Kanojo ni furareta koto ga aru n' da kara.*

A: So I go to take her hand, and she says "Cut it out."
But I'm sure it's just one of those cases where a
woman says no, but she really means yes, don't you
think?

B: Not her, you idiot. When she says "Forget it," she
means it. And I should know. 'Cause I've been
dumped by her before.

Sōsukan o kū 総すかんを食う To be given the cold shoulder by everyone; to be frozen out; to be in the doghouse.

➡ 彼は暴言を吐いて、総すかんを食った。

Kare wa bōgen o haite, sōsukan o kutta.

We all gave him the cold shoulder after he made that unbelievably stupid remark.

➡ この夏休みは旅行に行かないと言ったら、子供たちから総すかんを食った。

Kono natsuyasumi wa ryokō ni ikanai to ittara, kodomo-tachi kara sōsukan o kutta.

When I told the kids we weren't taking a trip this summer vacation, they all stopped speaking to me.

Mushizu ga hashiru 虫酸が走る Creepy; gives one the creeps [willies]; makes one shudder.

➥ あんな男といっしょに仕事をするなんて、思っただけで虫酸が走る。

Anna otoko to issho ni shigoto o suru nante, omotta dake de mushizu ga hashiru.

Just thinking about working with a guy like that gives me the willies.

➥ 彼がそばに来るだけで虫酸が走る。

Kare ga soba ni kuru dake de mushizu ga hashiru.

He just comes near me and it creeps me out.

Hakike ga suru 吐き気がする To dislike [someone or something] so much it makes one gag; to be unable to stand.

➥ あんないやらしい男、考えただけで吐き気がするほど大嫌い。

Anna iyarashii otoko, kangaeta dake de hakike ga suru hodo dai kirai.

Just thinking about that disgusting creep makes me want to gag.

Kegarawashii けがらわしい Foul; filthy; unclean.

➥ ほかの女を抱いた手で私にさわらないでよ、けがらわしい。

Hoka no onna o daita te de, watashi ni sawaranaide yo, kegarawashii.

Don't touch me with those hands you've been holding another woman with—how disgusting!

➥ 君がけがらわしい行為で手に入れたお金なんか、見るのもいやだ。

Kimi ga kegarawashii kōi de te ni ireta okane nanka, miru no mo iya da.

I don't even want to see the money you got doing such filthy things.

Hankan 反感 Antipathy; being opposed to; being offended by.

➡ 我々はボスのやりかたに反感を抱いた。

Wareware wa bosu no yarikata ni hankan o idaita.

We were opposed to the way the boss was doing things.

➡ 彼女の強引な売り込みは回りの人たちの反感を買った。

Kanojo no gōin na urikomi wa mawari no hitotachi no hankan o katta.

Her high-pressure sales tactics offended everyone around her.

Niramareru にらまれる Being marked by those in authority as one who needs watching; being watched.

➡ ぼくは学生運動の活動家だったから、大学当局からにらまれていた。

Boku wa gakusei-undō no katsudō-ka datta kara, daigaku-tōkyoku kara niramarete ita.

I was an activist in the student movement, so the school authorities kept an eye on me.

➡ 前に一度、ひどくたてついて以来、ぼくはあの課長ににらまれているらしい。

Mae ni ichido, hidoku tatetsuite irai, boku wa ano kachō ni niramarete iru rashii.

I once stood up quite defiantly to the section chief, and it seems he's been watching me ever since.

Me no kataki ni suru 目の敵にする To treat as an enemy; to act antagonistic toward.

➡ 彼はなにかというと、新入りの私を目の敵にする。

Kare wa nanika to iu to, shin'iri no watashi o me no kataki ni suru.

Whenever he gets a chance he treats me—the "new girl"—like the enemy.

(⚗ *Nanika to iu to* is a set phrase meaning whenever possible/whenever one gets a chance.)

➡ A: 「弘美って、私のこと目の敵にしているみたい」
   B: 「あの子、あなたと純のこと焼いてるのよ」

A: Hiromi tte, watashi no koto me no kataki ni shite iru mitai.

B: Ano ko, anata to Jun no koto yaite 'ru no yo.

A: Hiromi acts kind of antagonistic toward me.

B: She's just jealous about you and Jun.

Teki-i 敵意 Hostility; malice; animosity.

➡ 私の彼に気がある里美は、私に敵意をむき出しにしている。

Watashi no kare ni ki ga aru Satomi wa, watashi ni teki-i o mukidashi ni shite iru.

Satomi has designs on my boyfriend and isn't holding in any of the animosity she feels toward me.

➡ 先輩たちは僕に敵意を持っているらしい。

Senpai-tachi wa boku ni teki-i o motte iru rashii.

The older guys on the team seem to think of me as the enemy.

UNLIKABLE THINGS

Bu-aiso 不愛想 Unfriendly; curt; grumpy.

➡ あの寿司屋のおやじはお世辞ひとつ言わないで不愛想だが、腕は確かだ。

Ano sushi-ya no oyaji wa oseji hitotsu iwanai de bu-aiso da ga, ude wa tashika da.

The owner of that sushi shop is a grumpy sort who won't utter a word of flattery, but he sure can make sushi.

➡ 彼女は不愛想なんじゃなくて、初めてのアルバイトで緊張して笑顔が出ないだけなんだ。

Kanojo wa bu-aiso nan' ja nakute, hajimete no arubaito de kinchō shite egao ga denai dake nan da.

It's not that she's unfriendly, it's just that this is her first job and she's too nervous to smile.

Butchōzura 仏頂面 (Lit., "surface of top of Buddha's head) A sour face; a sullen expression; a grouchy look.

➡ 毎晩残業で帰りが遅いので女房は仏頂面をしている。

Maiban zangyō de kaeri ga osoi no de nyōbō wa bucchō-zura o shite iru.

I've been working overtime and getting home late every night, and my wife's being a real sourpuss about it.

➡ 朝5時に訪ねてこられたら、誰だって仏頂面するよ。

Asa goji ni tazunete koraretara, dare datte bucchōzura suru yo.

Who wouldn't look grouchy if you dropped in on them at five in the morning?

Niekiranai 煮え切らない Wishy-washy; noncommittal; indecisive; vacillating.

➡ 好きなのか嫌いなのかはっきりしてよ、煮え切らない人ね。

Suki na no ka kirai na no ka hakkiri shite yo, niekiranai hito ne.

Stop acting so wishy-washy! Do you like it or not?

➡ 会社は労災と認めることに対して煮え切らない態度なので、裁判に訴えるつもりだ。

Kaisha wa rōsai to mitomeru koto ni taishite niekiranai taido na no de saiban ni uttaeru tsumori da.

The company is waffling on whether to recognize the injury as work-related, so I intend to take it to court.

Ujiuji suru うじうじする Hesitant; [too] timid [to act].

➡ 気が弱くて彼女が好きだと言えずうじうじしているうちに、見限られてしまった。

Ki ga yowakute kanojo ga suki da to iezu ujiuji shite iru uchi ni, mikagirarete shimatta.

I was too shy to tell her I like her. I was still hemming and hawing when she gave up on me.

➡ うじうじした人は嫌い。だまっておれについて来いと言う人が好きよ。

Ujiuji shite hito wa kirai. Damatte ore ni tsuite koi to iu hito ga suki yo.

I hate guys who are unsure of themselves. I like the kind of guy who tells me to shut up and follow him.

Jibun-katte 自分勝手 (Lit., "self as one pleases") Self-centered; selfish; self-willed. (❀ The connotation of this phrase is negative. The emphasis here is on the fact that one ignores the wishes of others.)

➡ 団体旅行ですから、皆様、自分勝手な行動はお慎みください。

Dantai-ryokō desu kara, minasama, jibun-katte na kōdō wa otsusushimi kudasai.

This is a group tour, everyone, so please refrain from going off and doing whatever you might happen to feel like.

➡ 私のルームメートは自分の寝たい時には私が本を読んでいても、電気を消す自分勝手な人だ。

Watashi no rūmumēto wa jibun no netai toki ni wa watashi ga hon o yonde ite mo, denki o kesu jibun-katte na hito da.

My roommate's awfully self-centered. Whenever she wants to go to bed she just turns out the light, even if I should be reading a book.

Wagamama わがまま (Lit., "my way") Selfish; [wanting to have one's own way and not wanting to consider what others might want].

➡ 一人娘でチヤホヤされて育ったから彼女は人からわがままだと言われる。

Hitori musume de chiyahoya sarete sodatta kara kanojo wa hito kara wagamama da to iwareru.

As an only child, she was pampered growing up, and now people find her selfish.

➡ キャンプは集団生活だから、わがままを言ってはいけない。

Kyanpu wa shūdan-seikatsu da kara, wagamama o itte wa ikenai.

At summer camp we live together as a group, so don't try to have everything your own way.

Seikaku ga warui 性格が悪い (Lit., "character is bad")
Unsavory; not nice; just basically bad; nasty.

➨ 人の悪口ばかり言いふらすって、あいつ性格悪いよな。

Hito no waruguchi bakari iifurasu tte, aitsu seikaku warui yo na.

Nasty son of a bitch, isn't he? The way he goes around bad-mouthing people.

➨ 性格が悪いのって、直んないんじゃないの？

Seikaku ga warui no tte, nao'nnai n' ja nai no?

I doubt there's really any cure for someone who's just basically bad.

Konjō ga magatte iru 根性が曲がっている (Lit., "nature [disposition] is twisted") Cynical; perverse (not frank and open).

➨ せっかくの好意を疑うなんて、根性が曲がってるんじゃないの？

Sekkaku no kōi o utagau nante, konjō ga magatte 'ru n' ja nai no?

Isn't it kind of perverse to look for some ulterior motive behind a person's good will?

➨ 皮肉ばっかり言って、あんた、根性が曲がってるから嫌いよ！

Hiniku bakkari itte, anta, konjō ga magatte 'ru kara kirai yo.

I don't like you because you're so cynical. All you ever do is make sarcastic remarks!

➨ この根性曲がり！

Kono konjō magari!

You weasel!

Hikyō 卑怯 Cowardly; unmanly; mean; sneaky; unfair.

↝ 人の弱みに付け込むなんて、卑怯なやつだ。

Hito no yowami ni tsukekomu nante, hikyō na yatsu da.

He's a sneaky rat, taking advantage of people's weaknesses.

↝ 自分の失敗を人のせいにするなんて、卑怯なやつ！

Jibun no shippai o hito no sei ni suru nante, hikyō na yatsu!

Blaming others for your mistakes! You call yourself a man?

↝ なによ！今さら逃げるなんて卑怯者！

Nani yo! Imasara nigeru nante hikyō-mono!

You can't leave me now! Spineless bastard!

JEALOUSY

Netamu/netamashii 妬む/妬ましい   Jealous or envious.

↝ みどりは人気のある麻衣を妬んで、中傷しようとした。

Midori wa ninki no aru Mai o netande, chūshō shiyō to shita.

Midori was jealous of Mai for being so popular, and tried to spread nasty rumors about her.

↝ 少女たちは町でモデルにスカウトされた麗子を妬ましく思った。

Shōjo-tachi wa machi de moderu ni sukauto sareta Reiko o netamashiku omotta.

The girls were envious of Reiko, who was scouted off the street to work as a model.

Yakkamu やっかむ   To be envious or jealous; resent someone else's good fortune.

↝ 孝は賢二にすてきな恋人ができたのをやっかんでいる。

Takashi wa Kenji ni suteki na koibito ga dekita no o yakkande iru.

Takashi is envious of Kenji's having found such a foxy girlfriend.

➻ 妻：「小さい子どもを遠くの学校に通わせるなんてひどい親
　　　だって言われちゃった」
　　夫：「ほっとけよ。いい学校に入ったからやっかんでるんだよ」

Tsuma:　Chiisai kodomo o tōku no gakkō ni kayowaseru
　　　　　nante hidoi oya datte iwarechatta.

Otto:　　Hottoke yo. Ii gakkō ni haitta kara yakkande 'ru
　　　　　n' da yo.

Wife:　　She told me I was a rotten parent, for making a
　　　　　child his age commute so far to school.

Husband:　Don't let it get to you. She's just jealous be-
　　　　　cause he got into such a good school.

Urayamu/urayamashii　うらやむ/うらやましい　To
envy; to be jealous or envious (in a rather admiring, benign
way).

➻ 兄夫婦は人もうらやむ仲だ。

Ani-fūfu wa hito mo urayamu naka da.

People actually envy my brother and his wife for how well
they get along.

➻ 彼女の美貌がうらやましい。

Kanojo no bibō ga urayamashii.

I wish I had her looks.

Shitto　嫉妬　Jealousy; possessiveness.

➻ 私は小さいころ、いつもママにだっこされている妹に嫉妬
した。

*Watashi wa chiisai koro, itsumo mama ni dakko sarete iru
imōto ni shitto shita.*

When I was a child I was jealous of my younger sister for
always being held by my mother.

➻ うちの夫は嫉妬深い。

Uchi no otto wa shitto-bukai.

My husband is extremely jealous.

Yakimochi　焼もち　Jealousy; possessiveness.

➽ 彼女がきみに冷たくあたるのは、きっと焼もちを焼いているんだよ。

Kanojo ga kimi ni tsumetaku ataru no wa, kitto yakimochi o yaite iru n' da yo.

I'm sure that the reason she's so cold to you is that she's jealous.

➽ 焼もちもある程度ならいいけど……。

Yakimochi mo aru teido nara ii kedo ...

A certain amount of jealousy is all right, but ...

FIGHTING

Kenka けんか Fight; argument.

➽ A: 「今日もまた、チャーリーとけんかしちゃった」
  B: 「『けんかするほど仲がいい』なんて言うじゃない」

A: Kyō mo mata, Chārii to kenka shichatta.
B: "Kenka suru hodo naka ga ii" nante iu ja nai.

A: I had another fight with Charlie today.
B: Well, fighting is a sign of closeness, they say.

➽ 母親: 「お誕生日、はるかちゃんも呼ぶ？」
  男の子: 「いや、今けんかしてるんだから！」

Haha-oya: Otanjōbi, Haruka-chan mo yobu?
Otoko no ko: Iya, ima kenka shite 'ru n' da kara!

Mother: Do you want to invite Haruka-chan to your birthday [party]?
Little boy: No! Me and her are fighting right now!

Kyōdai-genka 兄弟げんか/姉妹げんか Fight [argument] between siblings.

➽ 娘: 「お母さん！お兄ちゃん、私のことぶった！」
  母親:「きょうだいげんかばっかりして！もっと仲良くできないの！？」

Musume: Okāsan! Oniichan, watashi no koto butta!

Haha-oya: Kyōdai-genka bakkari shite! Motto naka-yoku dekinai no!?

Daughter: Mom! He [older brother] hit me!

Mother: I swear, you two do nothing but fight! Can't you get along a little better?

Fūfu-genka 夫婦げんか Fight between a husband and a wife; a marital spat.

➥ A: 「隣の夫婦げんかは、派手だよね」
  B: 「うん、時々パトカーが来てるもんね」

A: Tonari no fūfu-genka wa, hade da yo ne.
B: Un, tokidoki patokā ga kite 'ru mon ne.

A: Those two next door really go at it, don't they?

B: I'll say. You even see cop cars there from time to time.

Urikotoba ni kaikotoba 売り言葉に買い言葉
(Lit., "the words of the seller, the words of the buyer.")
The hawker hawks and the buyer says "sold"—in other words, one reckless word leads to another.

This is a set phrase which suggests that in the heat of an argument it's easy to say something you will later regret—and not necessarily because you've hurt the other person's feelings.

➥ 彼が、嫌味ったらしく、「きみは、仕事が遅いね」なんて言うから、つい売り言葉に買い言葉で「冗談じゃない！今日中に終わるに決ってるでしょ！」なんて言っちゃったけど、どうしよう...

Kare ga, iyami ttarashiku, "Kimi wa, shigoto ga osoi ne" nante iu kara, tsui urikotoba ni kaikotoba de "Jōdan ja nai! Kyōjū ni owaru ni kimatte 'ru deshō!" nante itchatta kedo, dō shiyō ...

In a very nasty way he said, "You're awfully slow on the job, aren't you." Well, I shot right back at him with, "Don't be silly. I'll finish it all today for sure." Me and my big mouth!

Igami-au いがみ合う To feud; to engage in a long-running dispute.

➡ 彼らはピアノの音が原因で、いがみ合っている。

Karera wa piano no oto ga gen'in de, igami-atte iru.

It's a feud between neighbors: they're fighting over the noise from the piano.

➡ A:「あの二人の家は、代々いがみ合っているんだって」
　 B:「へえ、まるでロミオとジュリエットじゃない」

A: Ano futari no ie wa, daidai igami-atte iru n' datte.
B: Hē, maru de Romio to Jurietto ja nai.

A: The families of those two have been feuding for generations.

B: Cool. Just like Romeo and Juliet, eh?

Isakai いさかい Quarrel; conflict; argument.

➡ あの夫婦はいさかいがたえない。

Ano fūfu wa isakai ga taenai.

That couple's whole life is one long quarrel.

➡ わずかなお金の貸し借りが、いさかいの原因となった。

Wazuka na okane no kashikari ga, isakai no gen'in to natta.

The loan of a small amount of money wound up causing an argument.

Arasou 争う To fight, contend, or vie [for a prize].

➡ 女:「お願い！　二人とも私のために争うのは、やめて！」
　 男:「冗談じゃない！　負けたら、君と結婚しなきゃいけないんだよ！」

Onna: Onegai! Futari tomo watashi no tame ni arasou no wa, yamete!
Otoko: Jōdan ja nai! Maketara, kimi to kekkon shinakya ikenai n' da yo!

She: Please stop, both of you! Don't fight over me!
He: Are you kidding? Whoever loses has to marry you!

Kotsuniku no arasoi 骨肉の争い (Lit., "bone and blood fight") Fighting between relatives (usually over an inheritance).

➡ あの家では、父親の遺産をめぐって、骨肉の争いが起こっている。

Ano ie de wa, chichi-oya no isan o megutte, kotsuniku no arasoi ga okatte iru.

That family is squabbling over their father's estate.

DEFIANCE

Sakarau 逆らう To defy; to oppose; to disobey.

➡ おれに逆らうと、ろくなことはないからな！

Ore ni sakarau to, roku na koto wa nai kara na!

Cross me and you'll be sorry.

➡ あの人はうるさ型だから、逆らわないでなんでも「はい、はい」って聞いておく方が利口だよ。

Ano hito wa urusa-gata da kara, sakarawanai de nandemo "hai, hai" tte kiite oku hō ga rikō da yo.

That guy can be a real pain in the ass. You'd be wise not to contradict him—just agree to whatever he says.

Tatetsuku たて突く To defy someone in a position of authority.

➡ 何かというと部長にたて突いていた田中係長は、今度の人事移動で左遷された。

Nanika to iu to buchō ni tatetsuite ita Tanaka-kakarichō wa, kondo no jinji-idō de sasen sareta.

The chief clerk, Tanaka, who used to always stand up to the department manager, was demoted in the recent personnel reshuffling.

➡ 父親：「来週から、塾に行くんだよ」
息子：「お父さんがなんて言ったって、僕、塾なんか行かないよ」

父親: 「親にたて突くとは、なんだ！」

Chichi-oya: *Raishū kara, juku ni iku n' da yo."*

Musuko: *Otōsan ga nan te itta tte, boku, juku nanka ikanai yo.*

Chichi-oya: *Oya ni tatetsuku to wa, nanda!*

Father: Starting next week, you're going to cram school.

Son: I don't care what you say, I'm not going.

Father: How dare you speak to me that way!

Hankō suru 反抗する To rebel; to oppose; to defy; to not listen.

➡ 夫: 「うちの娘も、親に反抗するようになってしまったか……」
　妻: 「何言ってんの、おもちゃ取り上げたら、二歳児だって怒るに決まってるでしょ！」

Otto: *Uchi no musume mo, oya ni hankō suru yō ni natte shimatta ka …*

Tsuma: *Nani itte n' no, omocha toriagetara, nisai-ji datte okoru ni kimatte 'ru desho!*

Husband: So our daughter, too, has turned rebellious …

Wife: Get a grip. What two-year-old wouldn't throw a fit if you took away her toy?

➡ 若いころは誰でも親に反抗するものだ

Wakai koro wa dare de mo oya ni hankō suru mono da.

Everybody rebels against their parents when they're young.

Teikō suru 抵抗する To resist; to struggle; to oppose; to defy; to not act in accord with someone else's wishes.

➡ 彼女は必死で抵抗して、ひったくりからバッグを取り返した。

Kanojo wa hisshi de teikō shite, hittakuri kara baggu o tori-kaeshita.

She struggled desperately and managed to get her bag back from the purse-snatcher.

➡ 彼らは、抵抗もむなしく有り金すべてを奪い取られた。

Karera wa, teikō mo munashiku arigane subete o ubai to-rareta.

They resisted, but it was no use. They were robbed of all their money.

•• 会社が決めたことだから、抵抗してもしょうがないさ。

Kaisha ga kimeta koto da kara, teikō shite mo shō ga nai sa.

Hey, look, the company's made the decision, and it won't do you any good to put up a fight.

HATE

Nikumu 憎む To hate; to abhor; to detest; to despise.

•• 私の金をだまし取った男が憎い。

Watashi no kane o damashitotta otoko ga nikui.

I despise the man who conned me out of my money.

•• 彼は自分を裏切ったかつての親友を憎んでいる。

Kare wa jibun o uragitta katsute no shin'yū o nikunde iru.

He detests the old friend of his who betrayed him.

•• 彼女は、自分の気持ちを踏みにじった男に憎しみを抱くようになった。

Kanojo wa, jibun no kimochi o fuminijitta otoko ni niku-shimi o idaku yō ni natta.

She came to hate the guy who'd trampled all over her [feel-ings].

•• 私のことを「ババア！」だなんて、憎たらしいガキ！

Watashi no koto o "Babā!" da nante, nikutarashii gaki!

Despicable little brat! Calling me an old bag …

•• 私は戦争を憎む

Watashi wa sensō o nikumu.

I hate war.

•• あれは、私の弟をたぶらかした挙げ句自殺に追い込んだ、憎んでも憎みたりない女だ。

Are wa, watashi no otōto o taburakashita ageku jisatsu ni

oikonda, nikunde mo nikumitarinai onna da.

She's the woman whose deception of my younger brother drove him to suicide; my hatred for her has no bounds.

Imaimashii いまいましい Annoying; infuriating; vexing.

➡ 新人のくせに私より人気があるなんて、いまいましい。

Shinjin no kuse ni watashi yori ninki ga aru nante, ima-imashii.

It infuriates me that somebody new like her could be more popular than I am.

➡ 私の失敗を上司に言いつけるなんて、いまいましい奴だ。

Watashi no shippai o jōshi ni iitsukeru nante, imaimashii yatsu da.

What an annoying prick—telling the boss about my mistake.

Yatsuzaki ni suru 八つ裂きにする (Lit., "rip into eight pieces") To tear [someone] apart [from limb to limb]; to rip to shreds.

➡ 連続誘拐殺人の犯人は、八つ裂きにしても飽き足りない。

Renzoku yūkai satsujin no hannin wa, yatsuzaki ni shite mo akitarinai.

A serial kidnapper and murderer—drawing and quartering would be too good for him.

➡ あいつおれのせっかくの好意を無にしやがって、こんど会ったら八つ裂きにしてくれるわ。

Aitsu ore no sekkaku no kōi o mu ni shiyagatte, kondo at-tara yatsuzaki ni shite kureru wa.

Imagine that bastard turning down my kind offer! Next time I see him I'll tear him apart.

Bōzu nikukerya kesa made nikui 坊主憎けりゃ袈裟まで憎い ("If you hate the priest, you'll hate even his surplice") When you start to dislike someone, you begin to find even the inanimate objects associated with them repellent.

➡ 『坊主憎けりゃ袈裟まで憎い』のたとえ通り、あいつが好

きな歌さえ聞きたくなくなった。

"Bōzu nikukerya kesa made nikui" no tatoe-dōri, aitsu ga suki na uta sae kikitakunaku natta.

It's like that saying about the priest and his surplice—I don't even want to hear the songs he likes anymore.

➡ A: 「お隣さんと、けんかしたんだって？」
 B: 「まあね。それよりあの家の犬、やかましくて。水でもぶっ掛けてやろうかな」
 A: 「『坊主憎けりゃ袈裟まで……』だね」

A: *Otonarisan to, kenka shita n' datte?*
B: *Mā ne. Sore yori ano ie no inu, yakamashikute. Mizu demo bukkakete yarō ka na.*
A: *"Bōzu nikukerya kesa made …" da ne.*

A: You got in a fight with the neighbors?
B: I guess you could say that … Damn, their dog is noisy, though. Maybe I should give it a good dousing with water.
A: Sounds to me like a case of "hating even the surplice."

Nikumarekko yo ni habakaru 憎まれっ子世にはばかる "Hated ones prosper in this world"; "nice guys finish last"; "ill weeds grow apace"; "only the good die young."

➡ あの評論家、小学校の頃から嫌味な奴だった。「憎まれっ子世にはばかる」って本当だね。

Ano hyōron-ka, shō-gakkō no koro kara iyami na yatsu datta. "Nikumarekko yo ni habakaru" tte hontō da ne.

That critic was a disagreeable little twit even back in elementary school. It's true what they say—"Ill weeds grow apace."

➡ A: 「うちのお姑さん、嫌味で、いじわるで、近所でも嫌われてるんだから」
 B: 「『憎まれっ子、なんとやら……』で、長生きするよ」
 A: 「ああ、私の方が早死にしそう！」
 B: 「いや、君も結構長生きかも……」

A: *Uchi no oshūtome-san, iyami de, ijiwaru de, kinjo de mo kirawarete 'ru n' da kara.*

B: *"Nikumarekko, nan to yara" de, nagaiki suru yo.*

A: *Ā, watashi no hō ga hayaji ni shisō!*

B: *Iya, kimi mo kekkō nagaiki ka mo ...*

A: My mother-in-law is so unpleasant and mean that all the neighbors dislike her.

B: Well, they say only the good die young.

A: Oh, dear! I'll probably go before she does.

B: Nah, you might just live to a ripe old age yourself.

Zōo suru 憎悪する To feel an intense hatred.

➡ 私は、彼の卑劣なやり方を憎悪した。

Watashi wa, kare no hiretsu na yarikata o zōo shita.

I truly came to despise his sneaky ways.

➡ 彼女は、憎悪に燃えた目で夫の愛人をにらみつけた。

Kanojo wa, zōo ni moeta me de otto no aijin o niramitsuketa.

She gave her husband's mistress a look that was full of hatred.

SWEETLY TERRIBLE THINGS TO DO

Nikui is even stronger than *kirai* as an expression of displeasure or malice, yet it can sometimes have a positive connotation. The word can be used to call someone's behavior "terrible" in a coy, flirtatious way.

➡ 私をこんなに夢中にさせるなんて、あなたったら憎い人ね！

Watashi o konna ni muchū ni saseru nante, anata ttara nikui hito ne!

You've made me crazy about you, you naughty man.

➡ 誕生日にプロポーズなんて、憎い演出にころりと参っちゃった！！

Tanjōbi ni puropōzu nante, nikui enshutsu ni korori to maitchatta !!

It was a nasty trick, proposing on my birthday, and I fell like a ton of bricks.

●● 「課長のお人柄にほれて、入社を決めました」だなんて、お世辞にしたって憎いこと言ってくれるよな。

"Kachō no ohitogara ni horete, nyūsha o kimemashita" da nante, oseji ni shitatte nikui koto itte kureru yo na.

Section chief: "You said, 'I joined the company because I was so taken with your personality.' Flattery or not, that was a devilish thing to say!

HOLDING A GRUDGE

Uramu 恨む To bear a grudge; to resent; to blame.

●● 彼は、困っているときにしらんぷりをした人たちを恨んでいる。

Kare wa, komatte iru toki ni shiran-puri o shita hitotachi o urande iru.

He still holds a grudge against the people who couldn't be bothered to help when he was in trouble.

●● お岩は自分をだまして殺した男を恨んで化けて出た。

O-iwa wa jibun o damashite koroshita otoko o urande bakete deta.

O-iwa came back to haunt the man who'd deceived and murdered her.

●● 日本の幽霊は「うらめしや～」と言って出てくるらしい。

Nihon no yūrē wa "urameshiyā" to itte dete kuru rashii.

It seems that when Japanese ghosts appear, they say "urameshiyaaa," as an expression of their resentment and hatred.

Saka-urami suru 逆恨みする To bear a grudge against someone for no good reason, or in spite of the fact that they tried to be kind to one.

↠ 彼は自分がさぼってばかりいたくせに、落第させた学校に逆恨みをして放火した。

Kare wa jibun ga sabotte bakari ita kuse ni, rakudai saseta gakkō ni saka-urami o shite hōka shita.

He's the one who was always cutting class, but then when he flunked out he held it against the school and set the place on fire.

↠ A: 「雄太、勝手に私のこと好きになったくせに、私が好きじゃないって言ったら嫌がらせするのよ」

  B: 「逆恨みって恐いから、気を付けたほうがいいよ」

  A: Yūta, katte ni watashi no koto suki ni natta kuse ni, watashi ga suki ja nai tte ittara iyagarase suru no yo.

  B: Saka-urami tte kowai kara, ki o tsuketa hō ga iiyo.

  A: Yūta, with no encouragement on my part, decided he liked me. Now he's been harassing me just because I told him I didn't feel the same.

  B: You'd better be careful. People like that are dangerous sometimes.

Ne ni motsu 根に持つ Vindictive; spiteful; vengeful.

↠ 彼は、むかし君に人前でののしられたことをいまだに根に持っているよ。

Kare wa, mukashi kimi ni hitomae de nonoshirareta koto o imada ni ne ni motte iru yo.

He still holds it against you that you once bawled him out in front of the others.

↠ 彼女は、かなり根に持つタイプだ。

Kanojo wa, kanari ne ni motsu taipu da.

She's quite the vindictive type.

REVENGE

Ii kimi da いい気味だ (Lit., "good sensation") "Serves [someone] right" (used to express one's delight at seeing someone get their comeuppance).

➠ A: 「あのいじめっ子のウィリーが、犬にかまれてけがをしたんだって！」

　　B: 「いい気味だ、ざまあみろ！」

A: Ano ijimekko no Uirii ga, inu ni kamarete kega o shita n' datte!

B: Ii kimi da, zamā miro!

A: They tell me that little bully Willy was bitten pretty badly by a dog!

B: Good! Serves him right!

Sakaneji o kuwaseru 逆ねじをくわせる (Lit., "force-feed a reverse screw") Having the tables turned on one; the biter bit.

➠ 隣の犬がうるさいと文句を言いに行ったら、お宅の子供の方がもっとうるさいと逆ねじをくわされた。

Tonari no inu ga urusai to monku o ii ni ittara, otaku no kodomo no hō ga motto urusai to sakaneji o kuwasareta.

When I went to tell the neighbors their dog was making too much noise, they went me one better, saying that our kids were even noisier.

➠ 輸入規制に抗議したら、こちらが市場開放をしないからだと、逆ねじをくわされた。

Yunyū-kisei ni kōgi shitara, kochira ga shijō-kaihō o shinai kara da to, sakaneji o kuwasareta.

When we protested the restrictions on imports, they threw it back in our faces, saying that restrictions were necessary because we hadn't opened our markets.

Fukushū suru 復讐する To take revenge.

➠ 私にこんなひどい仕打ちをした彼に、いつかきっと復讐してやる。

Watashi ni konna hidoi shiuchi o shita kare ni, itsuka kitto fukushū shite yaru.

One day I swear I'll get him back for this terrible thing he did to me.

➡ 彼女は子供をひき逃げした犯人に復讐するためにだけ生きてきた。

Kanojo wa kodomo o hikinige shita hannin ni fukushū suru tame ni dake ikite kita.

She lives only for revenge against the hit-and-run driver who ran over her child.

BETRAYAL

Otoshiireru 陥れる   To entrap (someone); set (someone) up; land someone in trouble by deceiving them.

➡ 彼は、自分の出世のためなら、平気でライバルを陥れるような男だ。

Kare wa, jibun no shusse no tame nara, heiki de raibaru o otoshiireru yō na otoko da.

He's the sort of man who thinks nothing of playing dirty tricks on his rivals if it will further his own career.

Uragiru 裏切る   (Lit., "back cut") To betray; to stab in the back.

➡ A:「彼女だけは、僕を愛してくれているとばかり思っていたんだけどなあ……」
   B:「ぼくなんか、いつも女性に裏切られっぱなしさ」

A: Kanojo dake wa, boku o ai shite kurete iru to bakari o-motte ita n' dakedo nā ...

B: Boku nanka, itsumo josei ni urakirareppanashi sa.

A: And I was so sure of her, so sure that she, at least, loved me.

B: Hey, let me tell you, women are always betraying me.

➡ 人の信頼を裏切るようなことはするな。

Hito no shinrai o uragiru yō na koto wa suru na.

You must never betray a person's trust.

Negaeru 寝返る (Lit., "turn over in bed") To turn traitor; to change sides; to be a turncoat (often used in the political world).

◆ 副社長が急に寝返ってね、とうとう社長は退陣することになったよ。

Fuku-shachō ga kyū ni negaette ne, tōtō shachō wa taijin suru koto ni natta yo.

The deputy president suddenly turned against him, and the president finally just had to step down.

◆ 政治の世界では、いつ誰が寝返るか分からないですよ。

Seiji no sekai de wa, itsu dare ga negaeru ka wakaranai desu yo.

In the world of politics, you never who is going to change allegiances when.

Hameru はめる To entrap; to frame; to set [someone] up.

◆ 彼が左遷されたのは、同僚にはめられたからだ。

Kare ga sasen sareta no wa, dōryō ni hamerareta kara da.

The reason he was demoted was that his colleagues set him up.

◆ A: 「支店長、贈賄の容疑で調べられたらしいよ」
  B: 「異例の出世にやっかんだ奴がはめたっていう噂だよ」

A: Shiten-chō, zōwai no yōgi de shiraberareta rashii yo.
B: Irei no shusse ni yakkanda yatsu ga hameta tte uwasa da yo.

A: I understand they investigated the branch manager for corruption.
B: But they say he was framed by somebody who was jealous of the way he moved up so quickly.

Nieyu o nomaseru 煮え湯を飲ませる (Lit., "made to drink boiling water") Describes the heartbreak of having one's confidence betrayed by, or of being deceived by, someone one cares about

➻ ビルは、可愛がっていた部下に裏切られて、煮え湯を飲ま された思いだった。

Biru wa, kawaigatte ita buka ni uragirarete, nieyu o no-maserareta omoi datta.

It broke Bill's heart when he was betrayed by a subordinate he was particularly fond of.

HORRIBLE THINGS

Zotto suru ぞっとする   To shudder with horror; to have the creeps; to get goosebumps [gooseflesh].

➻ あんな男に触られたらぞっとするわ！

Anna otoko ni sawararetara zotto suru wa!

It would give me the creeps if a man like that touched me!

➻ 私が乗るはずだった飛行機が不時着炎上したと聞き、ぞっ とした。

Watashi ga noru hazu datta hikōki ga fujichaku enjō shita to kiki, zotto shita.

A chill ran right through me when I heard that the airplane I was supposed to be on had made a crash landing and burned.

Samuke ga suru 寒気がする   Chilling; makes one's blood run cold; sends shivers down one's spine (the sense of repulsion here is even stronger than that of *zotto suru.*).

➻ 毎日、家の前でしつこく僕を待ち伏せている女には寒気 がするよ。

Mainichi, ie no mae de shitsukoku boku o machibuse shite iru onna ni wa samuke ga suru yo.

The woman who hangs around out in front of my house every day, waiting for me to come out, sends shivers down my spine.

●→ ごく微量で何千人も殺せる能力のある薬が発明されたと聞
き、寒気を覚えた。

*Goku biryō de nan-zennin mo koroseru kōryoku no aru
kusuri ga hatsumei sareta to kiki, samuke o oboeta.*

When I heard they'd invented a poison so strong that the
tiniest bit could kill thousands of people, my blood ran cold.

Ozomashii おぞましい　Inhumanly cruel; unspeakable;
horrific.

●→ 幼児連続誘拐殺人のようなおぞましい事件は、二度と起こ
してはならない。

*Yōji renzoku yūkai satsujin no yō na ozomashii jiken wa,
nido to okoshite wa naranai.*

Incidents such as this string of infant kidnap-murders are
an unspeakable outrage that we must never allow to occur
again.

●→ 戦争中のおぞましい光景を写真で見て心が痛んだ。

*Sensō-chū no ozomashii kōkei o shashin de mite kokoro ga
itanda.*

I got depressed looking at photographs of these horrible
scenes from the war.

WE'VE BEEN THROUGH
A LOT TOGETHER!
NOW LET'S BREAK UP!

Ii otomodachi de imashō　いいお友達でいましょう
("Let's be good friends") A gentle way to tell someone you
aren't interested in getting romantically involved. (⚥ Most
commonly used by women.)

●→ A：「彼女に恋人になってほしいって言ったら、『いいお友達
でいましょう』だって。彼女も僕のこと嫌いじゃなかっ
たんだ」

B: 「ばかだなあ、それ、ふられたってことだよ」

A: *Kanojo ni koibito ni natte hoshi tte ittara, "Ii otomo-dachi de imashō" datte. Kanojo mo boku no koto kirai ja nakatta n' da.*

B: *Baka da nā, sore, furareta tte koto da yo.*

A: When I asked her to be my girl, she goes, "Let's be good friends." So I guess she likes me too!

B: What are you, an idiot? You've been dumped, man.

Sameru 冷める (Lit., "get cold") To stop loving; to fall out of love with; to grow cold toward.

‣ 彼に対する気持ちはすっかり冷めてしまった。

Kare ni taisuru kimochi wa sukkari samete shimatta.

My feelings for him have completely died.

‣ 愛は冷めているのに、離婚しない夫婦はいくらでもいる。

Ai wa samete iru no ni, rikon shinai fūfu wa ikura de mo iru.

There are any number of couples who remain married even when they no longer have any feelings for each other.

Suteru 捨てる (Lit., "throw away") To dump; to break up with.

‣ 彼は出世に目がくらみ、私を捨てて社長の娘と結婚した。

Kare wa shusse ni me ga kurami, watashi o sutete shachō no musume to kekkon shita.

Blinded by ambition, he dumped me and married the CEO's daughter.

‣ A: 「昔の恋人から10年ぶりに電話があって、お金を貸してほしいって言うのよ。なんだかすごく困っているみたいだった」

B: 「なに言ってんの！あなたを捨てた男じゃないの！」

A: *Mukashi no koibito kara jūnen-buri ni denwa ga atte, okane o kashite hoshii tte iu no yo. Nandaka sugoku ko-matte iru mitai datta.*

B: *Nani itte n' no! Anata o suteta otoko ja nai no!*

A: My old boyfriend called me for the first time in ten years and asked me to lend him some money. It seems he's in a terrible fix, so …

B: What are you talking about! This is a guy who dumped you!

Furu ふる To reject [someone's advances]; to refuse [a date]; to turn [someone] down; to break up with.

➡ 家柄も財産も学歴も申しぶんないし、そのうえあんなハンサムで優しい人をふるなんて、一体どこが気に入らなかったの？

Iegara mo zaisan mo gakureki mo mōshibun nai shi, sono ue anna hansamu de yasashii hito o furu nante, ittai doko ga ki ni iranakatta no?

He's from a good family, he's got money, and he's well educated, on top of which he's good-looking and also nice as can be, yet you turn him down [break up with him]—what didn't you like about him?

➡ 彼女を映画に誘ったら、先約があるってふられちゃったよ。

Kanojo o eiga ni sasottara, sen'yaku ga aru tte furare-chatta yo.

I asked her out to a movie, but she blew me off. Said she had a previous engagement.

Sode ni suru 袖にする To give [someone] the cold shoulder; to ignore; to jilt; to walk out on.

➡ 私は、彼に袖にされたことを恨んでいる。

Watashi wa, kare ni sode ni sareta koto o urande iru.

I resent him for giving me the cold shoulder.

➡ あんないい女を袖にするなんて、罰が当たるぞ。

Anna ii onna o sode ni suru nante, bachi ga ataru zo.

Walking out on such a fine woman. God'll punish you, brother.

Wakareru 別れる To split up with; to break up with; to separate; to divorce.

➡ 彼女は夫と別れた。

Kanojo wa otto to wakareta.

She and her husband divorced.

➡ 彼は恋人と別れてから、しばらく女性不信に陥った。

Kare wa koibito to wakarete kara, shibaraku josei fushin ni ochiitta.

He distrusted all women for a while after he and his girl-friend split up.

Kane no kireme ga en no kireme 金の切れ目が縁の切れ目 "When the money's finished, the relationship's finished."

➡ A: 「彼と別れちゃった。だって、このごろ何にも買ってくれないんだもの」
　 B: 「金の切れ目が縁の切れ目って言うもんね」

A: *Kare to wakarechatta. Datte, konogoro nani ni mo katte kurenai n' da mono.*

B: *Kane no kireme ga en no kireme tte iu mon ne.*

A: I broke up with him. Can you blame me? He hasn't bought me a thing lately!

B: Like they say, "when the wolf comes in at the door, love creeps out of the window!"

PROVERBS AND SAYINGS
✢
ABOUT HUSBANDS AND WIVES

● **Omae hyaku made washa kujuku made (tomo ni shiraga no haeru made)**

おまえ百までわしゃ九十九まで、共に白髪の生えるまで

"Till you're one hundred and I'm ninety-nine, together till our hair grows white ..." (A set phrase, often used in wedding banquet speeches and the like, expressing the hope that a couple will have a long, happy life together.)

● **Teishu kanpaku**

亭主関白

"The husband is king of his castle"

● **Naijo no kō**

内助の功

"With the wife's help" (Behind every good man there's a good woman.)

● **Fūfu-genka wa inu mo kuwanai**

夫婦げんかは犬も食わない

"Even dogs find marital spats unpalatable" (Dogs will eat anything, but even they keep their noses out of marital spats. Fights between husbands and wives arise and are settled again so easily that it's best for other people to keep their noses out.)

● **Fūfu-genka wa binbō no tane-maki**

夫婦げんかは貧乏の種蒔き

"Marital discord sows the seeds of poverty" (When husband and wife don't get along well, the man is likely to turn to drink and debauchery and the woman to wasteful spending—which in turn, of course, can lead to financial ruin.)

- **Fūfu wa nise no chigiri**

夫婦は二世の契り

"Marriage is a vow for two worlds" (The ties that bind a married couple are so strong that they hold even after death—in the "other world.")

- **Fushō fuzui**

夫唱婦随

"The husband leads [chants], the wife follows [obeys]" (The secret to a happy marriage.)

- **Nomi no fūfu**

ノミの夫婦

"Husband and wife fleas" (A couple in which the man is smaller than the woman.)

- **Nitamono fūfu**

似た者夫婦

"Like husband, like wife" (A couple whose personalities and interests are similar; also, a couple who have come to resemble each other over time.)

- **Warenabe ni tojibuta**

割れ鍋に綴じ蓋

"A lid to fit a cracked pot"; every pot has its cover"; there's someone [a good match] for everyone.)

ABOUT BRIDES AND MOTHERS-IN-LAW

- **Akinasu wa yome ni kuwasu na**

秋茄子は嫁に食わすな

"Don't feed a bride autumn eggplant" (Since eggplant picked in autumn is considered a delicacy, it was traditionally thought to be too good for the lowly daughter-in-law.)

● **Yome to shūtome, inu to saru**

嫁と姑、犬と猿

"Bride and mother-in-law: monkey and dog" (Monkeys and dogs, according to Japanese tradition, do not get along. This, of course, is traditionally true of brides and mothers-in-law as well.)

● **Yome ni kojūto oni senbiki**

嫁に小姑鬼千匹

"To the bride, the sister-in-law is a thousand demons" (For the bride, the sister-in-law too is traditionally a mean and fearsome person.)

● **Yome no rusu wa shūtome no shōgatsu**

嫁の留守は姑の正月

"The bride's absence is the mother-in-law's New Year's" (The mother-in-law is relaxed and happy when the bride is not at home.)

● **Yome wa shūtome ni niru**

嫁は姑に似る

"The bride resembles the mother-in-law" (The bride and mother-in-law may not get along well at first, but over time the younger woman eventually begins to take on many of the ways of the older.)

● **Yome wa nikui ga mago wa kawaii**

嫁は憎いが孫は可愛い

"The bride is hateful, but the grandchild is sweet"

ABOUT PARENTS AND CHILDREN

● **Itsumademo aru to omou na oya to kane**

いつまでもあると思うな親と金

"Two things that don't last forever: parents and money"

● **Umi no oya yori sodate no oya**

生みの親より育ての親

"Foster parents are dearer than birth parents"

● **Kōkō o shitai toki ni wa oya wa nashi**

孝行をしたい時には親はなし

"By the time you realize how much you owe them, you have no parents left to repay"

● **Kodomo no kenka ni oya ga deru**

子供のけんかに親が出る

"Parents sticking their noses into children's spats" (An admonition to parents to let children make their own way. Fighting is a natural part of learning to get along with others.)

● **Ko wa oya o utsusu kagami**

子は親を映す鏡

"A child is a mirror that reflects the parent"

● **Nasubi no hana to oya no iken wa, sen ni hitotsu no muda mo nai**

茄子の花と親の意見は、千に一つの無駄もない

"Eggplant flowers and parents' opinions: not one in a thousand is without its uses"

● **Oya-omou kokoro ni masaru oyagokoro**

親思う心にまさる親心

"The parent's love exceeds the child's"

● **Haeba tate, tateba ayume no oyagokoro**

這えば立て、立てば歩めの親心

"Crawling? 'Stand!' Standing? 'Walk!' Such is parental affection" (A depiction of the hopefulness and impatience parents feel as they watch their children develop)

● Baka na ko hodo kawaii

馬鹿な子ほどかわいい

"No child so adorable as a foolish one" (Used in a broad variety of situations, this phrase suggests that the child—or any other project—requiring a lot of attention makes the person in charge of it feel important and, therefore, happy.)

● Oya no kokoro ko shirazu

親の心子知らず

"Children don't know parents' hearts" (Children don't realize how much their parents love them.)

● Oya no nana-hikari

親の七光り

"The benefit of the parents' power and influence" (A metaphorical expression for nepotism. Used dismissively to suggest that someone's success is not the result of their own doing but of a parent's power or influence.)

Index

日本語の感情表現集
LOVE, HATE AND EVERYTHING
IN BETWEEN

1997年 4 月 1 日　第 1 刷発行

著　者　　村上真美子

発行者　　野間佐和子

発行所　　講談社インターナショナル株式会社
　　　　　〒112 東京都文京区音羽 1-17-14
　　　　　電話：03-3944-6493

印刷所　　株式会社　平河工業社

製本所　　株式会社　堅省堂

落丁本・乱丁本は、小社営業部宛にお送りください。送料
小社負担にてお取替えします。本書の無断複写（コピー）、
転載は著作権法の例外を除き、禁じられています。

定価はカバーに表示してあります。
© 講談社インターナショナル 1997
Printed in Japan
ISBN4-7700-2089-9